Girl's Skills
for Life

Solange Márquez

Original Title: GIRL'S SKILLS FOR LIFE
First edition: DEC. 2023

© 2023 SOLANGE MÁRQUEZ ESPINOZA

E-Book ISBN: 978-1-7381701-1-1
Printed Book: 978-1-7381701-0-4
Hardcover Book ISBN: 978-1-7381701-2-8

To Paco, the cornerstone of my life., my partner, my confidant, my everything. In every step, challenge, and moment, both joyous and trying, your presence has been a constant source of strength and happiness. Together, in this life and whatever may follow.

To Aysel and Shani, for gracing my life with the gift of your trust and presence. Your choice to walk this path with us has filled my world with immeasurable joy and completeness.

TABLE OF CONTENTS

1

INTRODUCTION

Hey there, awesome girls! Welcome to "Girl's Skills for Life," your super-cool guide to discovering and mastering all sorts of amazing skills. As a proud mom of Aysel and Shani, two incredibly curious and kind daughters, I'm thrilled to take you on this fun-filled journey. Together, we'll learn, explore, and grow into even more incredible versions of yourselves.

Much of this book was inspired by the adventures and plans I've shared with Aysel and Shani. I learned many of these skills later in life and wish I had known them as a young girl. They would have helped me become a more confident woman. But it's never too late to learn, and now, it fills me with immense joy to pass these skills on to my daughters and now to you.

In this book, we'll dive into everything from whipping up yummy treats in the kitchen to becoming a money-saving superstar. You'll crack the code of STEM, unleash your inner artist, and even become a confident leader. And guess what? You'll also hear about our own real-life adventures! My daughters, their dad Paco, and I – a family that's less than perfect but always eager to learn, improve, and find happiness together every single day – have had a blast mastering these skills, and we can't wait to share our stories with you.

But hold on, there's more! We'll venture into the great outdoors for some unforgettable camping and stargazing, unravel the mysteries of detective work, and capture the world's beauty through photography. This handbook is more than just lessons; it's a celebration of curiosity, bravery, and all the beautiful things you're capable of achieving.

So, are you ready to embark on this adventure with us? Let's fill these pages with joy, discovery, and memories to last a lifetime. Together, we'll laugh, learn, and leap into new experiences. It's time to turn the first page of your very own handbook to life, a journey that's as unique and special as you are. Let's make it an adventure to remember!

CHAPTER ONE

SUPER SKILLS FOR HOME AND BEYOND

We start our journey by going into some essential skills that you'll find not just helpful but also fun and empowering. As we begin, let me share some of my favorite tips and tricks for mastering basic survival and home skills. These skills will help you become more independent and give you a sense of accomplishment.

COOKING TIME!

Let's start in the heart of the home: the kitchen. Cooking is a fantastic skill. It's about creativity, understanding nutrition, and sharing love and care through what we eat. Aysel, Shani, and I often explore simple recipes together (it's also our bonding time). From cracking an egg to making a simple pasta dish, I'll walk you through each step. We'll also talk about kitchen safety, a lesson I emphasize with Aysel and Shani, like handling knives and keeping the cooking space clean. And yes, we'll cover how to use appliances safely, including the microwave. Shani loves to set the timer and watch as the ingredients transform!

Our journey begins in the kitchen. We'll start with some basics for beginners, and I'll walk you through each step, from learning how to crack an egg to making a fruit salad. You'll learn the essentials of kitchen safety, such as handling knives correctly, understanding the importance of cleanliness, and using appliances like the toaster responsibly. These skills will make you self-reliant and instill confidence as you navigate your way around the kitchen, preparing simple yet satisfying meals.

ESSENTIALS OF KITCHEN SAFETY

First things first, safety is super important in the kitchen, just like in a superhero's training ground. Then, we will talk about using a knife, the heat, keeping things clean, and using kitchen appliances, like the microwave, responsibly. So, let's dive in!

USING A KNIFE

1. Adult Supervision: This is super important. Always have an adult around when you're using a knife.
2. Choosing the Right Knife: A small or medium-sized kitchen knife will do most of your cutting. The big ones can wait until you're a bit older.
3. Grip and Control: Hold the knife firmly by the handle. Never put your fingers on the blade.
4. Cutting: Always cut away from your body. Keep your fingers away from the blade as you slice. Move slowly and steadily.
5. Focus: Always keep your eyes on the knife when it's in your hand. No looking away!

USING HEAT

1. Adult Supervision: Always ask your parents to be with you when you're using the stove.
2. Handling Pots and Pans: When you put a pot or pan on the stove, ensure the handle is turned away from the edge. This way, no one can accidentally bump into it.
3. Managing the Heat: Start with a low or medium heat. High heat can be tricky and is often optional.
4. Stirring and Flipping: When you stir or flip something in a pan, do it gently. This way, you won't get splashed by hot food or oil.

USING A TOASTER

1. Adult Supervision: Again, toasters can be dangerous, so be sure to get permission and adult supervision when using them.
2. Start with a Clean Workspace: Ensure the area around the toaster is clear of any clutter, liquids, or flammable items like paper towels or curtains.
3. Plug in the Toaster: First, make sure your hands are dry. Then plug in the toaster into a power outlet. Always ensure the toaster is off or on a minimal setting before plugging it in.

4. Adjust the Toaster Settings: Most toasters have a dial to control how brown you want your toast. Start with a lower setting. You can always toast your bread more if it's not as crispy as you like.
5. Insert the Bread: Open the toaster slots and carefully place your bread into them. Make sure to avoid cramming the bread in; it should fit easily.
6. Push Down the Lever: Once your bread is in, push down the lever on the side of the toaster. The bread will go down, and the heating process will start.
7. Stay Nearby: Stay close to the toaster while your bread is toasting. Never leave it unattended.
8. Wait for the Toast to Pop Up: The toaster will make a 'pop' sound, and the toast will come up when it's done. If it doesn't pop up, the toast may need more time. But never use a fork or knife to check on your toast – this can be very dangerous!
9. Remove the Toast Safely: Let the toast cool down briefly once the toast pops up. Then, gently remove it from the toaster. Be careful, as the toast and the toaster will be hot.
10. Unplug the Toaster: After you're done, unplug the toaster. This is an important safety step.
11. Cleaning: If there are crumbs, wait until the toaster is completely cool. Some toasters have a crumb tray at the bottom – slide it out and dispose of the crumbs.
6.

> Note: Toasters can get very hot, so handling them carefully is always essential

CLEANLINESS AND WASTE REDUCTION

Washing your hands before and after handling food is like having your very own magic shield against germs. Keeping your workspace clean is not just neat; it's safe and makes you feel like a professional chef!

Aysel and Shani have become champions of the environment in our kitchen. They've learned the importance of separating waste into recycling, organic, and inorganic bins, and we also have talked about reducing food waste. Did you know that saving leftovers can be a fun challenge? Figuring out how to use them in new and tasty ways is like a puzzle!

USING APPLIANCES RESPONSIBLY

1. The Microwave: Microwaves are super handy, but remember, metal and microwaves are not friends. Never put anything metal (like forks or aluminum foil) inside the microwave. Use microwave-safe containers and always follow the instructions for cook times.
2. The Oven and Stove: Always ask for an adult's help when using the oven or stove. They can get really hot and need careful handling. When you're older, you'll learn to use these all by yourself, but for now, teaming up with an adult is the best way.
3. Electrical Safety: Keep electrical appliances, like blenders or toasters, away from water. Electricity and water are a dangerous mix. Always dry your hands before using these appliances.
4. Hot Surfaces: Pot handles and oven doors can be hot! When opening the oven door or handling hot pots, use oven mitts.

Being safe in the kitchen is just as crucial as making yummy food. By following these simple safety tips and being mindful of our environment, you'll become a responsible, skilled, and environmentally conscious young chef. So, let's keep it clean, safe, and fun in the kitchen!

LET'S COOK!

Now that we've covered the essentials of kitchen safety, it's time to put on our chef hats and dive into the fun part: cooking! In this section, we'll turn our safe, clean kitchen into a playground of flavors and creativity. Whether you're cracking your first egg or mixing up your favorite pasta dish, each recipe here is designed to make cooking feel like a delightful discovery. So, roll up your sleeves, put on your apron, and start this delicious journey. Are you ready to whip up some magic in the kitchen? Let's get cooking!

CRACKING AN EGG

Okay, let's start with something that might seem tricky at first, but I promise you'll get the hang of it quickly. We're going to crack an egg! It's a fundamental skill in cooking, and once you master it, you'll feel like a pro. I remember how Aysel and Shani giggled the first time they tried it, and the egg ended up a bit everywhere.

But soon, they mastered the art, and now they can do it with their eyes closed! Well, almost.

1. Find a Flat Surface: It might be your kitchen counter or a large cutting board. Avoid using the mouth of the plate you are using.
2. Hold the Egg Gently: Pick up an egg and hold it in one hand. Be gentle, as eggs are delicate.
3. Give It a Firm Tap: Aim for a slight crack, not too hard, or it might smash.
4. Use Your Thumbs: Gently push into the crack and pull the eggshell apart over a bowl.
5. Check for Shell Bits: If any sneak in, scoop it out with a larger piece of eggshell or with a spoon.

And there you have it! Cracking an egg might seem a bit scary at first, but with practice, it's as easy as pie.

RECIPES!

Scrambled Eggs

This simple yet delightful dish is packed with protein and can be jazzed up with your favorite ingredients like cheese or herbs.

Ingredients: 2 eggs, salt, 1 tbsp of milk (optional), butter or oil for the pan.

Steps:

1. Crack the eggs into a bowl.
2. Add a pinch of salt and milk (just a bit might get your scrambled eggs creamier). Beat the eggs until thoroughly mixed.
3. Heat a non-stick pan over low/medium heat. Add butter or oil, not too much!
4. Pour in the eggs once the butter is melted or the oil is heated.
5. Let the eggs sit for a moment, then stir, pushing the eggs from the edges to the center.
6. Continue until the eggs are fully cooked but still moist. Remove from heat and serve.
7.

> Cooking Tip: For fluffier scrambled eggs, cook them on low heat and be patient. It's worth the wait!

Classic Sandwich

Ingredients: Bread slices, ham or turkey, cheese slice, lettuce, tomato, mayonnaise, or mustard.

Steps:

1. Lay out two slices of bread.
2. Spread a layer of mayonnaise on one slice of bread and mustard on the other.
3. Place a slice of ham or turkey on top.
4. Add a slice of cheese.
5. Place a slice of tomato and lettuce on top.
6. Cover with the second slice of bread. Cut the sandwich in half if desired.
8.

- Peanut Butter and Jelly Sandwich

Ingredients: Bread slices, peanut butter, jelly, or jam.

Steps:

1. Lay out two slices of bread.
2. Spread peanut butter on one slice.
3. Spread jam or jelly on the other slice.
4. Press the two slices together. Cut the sandwich in half if desired.

Fruit Salad

A delicious mix of your favorite fruits can be a refreshing treat. It's full of vitamins and natural sugars, making it a healthy, sweet option.

Ingredients: A selection of fruits (e.g., bananas, apples, grapes, berries), honey or yogurt (optional).

Steps:

1. Wash and prepare the fruits.
2. Mix all the fruits in a large bowl.
3. If desired, add honey or yogurt for extra flavor.
4. Stir gently to combine.

- Pasta Dish

Ingredients: Pasta, salt, water, pre-made pasta sauce, grated cheese (optional).

Steps:

1. Fill a pot with enough water, add a pinch of salt, and bring it to a boil over low/medium heat.
2. When the water is boiling, add the pasta.
3. Cook using the times marked on the package instructions (usually about 8-10 minutes for al dente).
4. Carefully drain the pasta in a colander.
5. Return the pasta to the pot and stir in the pre-made sauce.
6. Heat it through.
7. Serve with grated cheese if desired.

- Microwave Chocolate Oatmeal Cookies

Ingredients:

- o 1/4 cup milk
- o 1/4 cup unsalted butter
- o 1/3 cup granulated sugar.
- o 1 1/2 tablespoons unsweetened cocoa powder
- o 1/4 cup peanut butter
- o One teaspoon of vanilla extract
- o 1 1/2 cups quick-cooking oats
- o Wax paper or a silicone baking mat

Steps:

1. Mix Wet Ingredients: In a microwave-safe bowl, combine milk, butter, sugar, and cocoa powder. This will be the base of your cookies.
2. Microwave the Mixture: Microwave the bowl on high for about 90 seconds. Then remove the bowl from the microwave (it might be hot, so you might need an adult to help or use oven mitts). Stir the mixture well until it's smooth.
3. Add Peanut Butter and Vanilla: Add the peanut butter and vanilla extract to the bowl. Stir everything until the peanut butter is fully melted and the mixture is well combined.
4. Mix in the Oats: Add the quick-cooking oats to your chocolate mixture. Stir until all oats are coated and everything is well mixed.
5. Shape the Cookies: Lay a wax paper on a flat surface. Using a spoon, drop a spoonful of the cookie mixture onto the wax paper. You can shape them a little with the back of the spoon to make them round.
6. Chill the Cookies: Let the cookies cool at room temperature for about 20 minutes, or put them in the fridge to set faster. They will harden as they cool.
7. Enjoy: Once the cookies are set and firm, they are ready to eat. Enjoy your homemade no-bake cookies!

Note: Always be careful when handling hot ingredients and appliances. It's a good idea to have an adult nearby to help with the microwave and take the hot bowl.

Trivia Time: Did you know that the tomato is technically a fruit, not a vegetable? But in cooking, it's usually treated as a vegetable due to its savory flavor!

FASHION CARE

Alright, after mastering some kitchen skills, let's switch gears to another super important life skill: doing laundry! It might not sound as exciting as cooking, but trust me, knowing how to wash and care for your clothes is just as rewarding. Let's dive into using the washer and dryer safely and effectively, taking care of the environment simultaneously.

USING THE WASHER

1. Sorting Clothes: Always check the care label. Some clothes require hand washing or specific settings. Divide clothes by color: dark, white, and red.

2. Checking Pockets: Always check your pockets! Forgotten items like tissues or coins can make a mess in the wash.
3. Setting Up the Washer: Add the clothes and the right amount of laundry detergent. Opt for environmentally friendly detergents that are kinder to the planet.
4. Selecting the Right Cycle: Different clothes need different settings. Choose the appropriate setting. Delicate, regular, and heavy-duty are standard options. When in doubt, the regular cycle is usually a safe bet. Using cold water for washing can save energy and is often as effective as hot.
5. Starting the Machine: Close the lid or door and press the start button. Now, the washer will do its magic!

HAND WASHING DELICATES

1. Fill a Basin: For clothes needing hand washing, fill a basin with water (better if it is warm) and add detergent.
2. Gentle Wash: Submerge and gently swish the garment, then let it soak.
3. Rinse and Dry: Rinse under cold water. Gently squeeze out excess water (don't wring!) and lay it flat to dry.

USING THE DRYER

1. Check for Heat-Sensitive Clothes: Some clothes can't handle the heat of a dryer and need to air dry. Always check the tags on your clothes for instructions.
2. Clean the Lint Trap: Before putting on clothes, clean the lint trap. It's a little drawer or shelf right inside the dryer door. Pull it out and remove the lint. This helps your dryer work better and prevents fire hazards.
3. Load the Dryer: Transfer your wet clothes from the washer to the dryer. Don't overload it; the clothes need room to tumble around.
4. Select the Right Heat Setting: Dryers have different settings, like the washer. Use a lower heat for delicate items and a higher heat for towels or sheets.
5. Start the Dryer: Close the door, press the start button, and let the dryer do its work.
6. Remove Clothes Promptly: Once the cycle is done, take your clothes out promptly to prevent wrinkles.

Doing laundry isn't just about clean clothes; it's about learning responsibility and independence. Aysel and Shani, for example, have their laundry schedule. They know when it's their turn to do laundry, and they take charge of their clothes. They've even turned laundry time into fun time, bringing their favorite music to the laundry room and singing as they sort and fold. It's never boring with them around!

THE LAUNDRY GAME!

To make laundry more fun, try the Laundry Game! As you sort your clothes, pretend you're a fashion designer organizing fabrics for your next big runway show. When folding clothes, see how neatly you can stack them. Imagine you're setting up a display in a high-end boutique. Who says laundry can't be glamorous?

If you're unsure about how to wash a particular item, it's always okay to ask for help and make sure there's an adult nearby the first few times you do laundry. Happy washing, drying, and singing!

DISH WASHING

After conquering laundry, let's dive into another essential skill: dishwashing! Whether you're hand washing dishes or using a dishwasher, keeping your dishes clean is not just about sparkle; it's about hygiene and caring for your environment. Let's scrub in!

HAND WASHING DISHES

1. Gather Your Supplies: You'll need environmentally friendly soap, a scrub brush or sponge, and a drying rack or towel.
2. Scrape Off Leftovers: Remove leftover food into the trash or compost bin before washing.
3. Fill the Sink: Plug the sink and fill it with warm, soapy water instead of letting it run continuously. This helps save water.
4. Scrub-a-Dub-Dub: Submerge your dishes in the water and scrub them with the sponge or brush, starting with the least dirty items and ending with the dirtiest.
5. Rinse and Dry: Rinse each item under running water to remove soap suds, then place them on the drying rack or dry with a towel.

USING THE DISHWASHER

1. Scrape Off Leftovers: Remove leftover food into the trash or compost bin.
2. Rinse Dishes First: A quick rinse can remove large food particles before loading.
3. Load Smartly: Put glasses and mugs on the top rack and plates and bowls on the bottom. Ensure nothing blocks the spray arms.
4. Eco-Friendly Detergent: Use environmentally friendly dishwasher detergent.
5. Full Loads: Run the dishwasher only when it's full to conserve water and energy.
6. Set the Cycle: Choose the proper cycle for your load. The normal cycle works for most needs.
7. Unloading the Dishwasher: Empty the bottom rack first to avoid drips from the top dishes.

EFFICIENCY TIPS

- Soak Pots and Pans: If you have heavily soiled pots and pans, let them soak before washing to make scrubbing easier.
- Right Amount of Detergent: Use just enough detergent to clean your dishes effectively. Overuse can lead to extra suds and residue.

Doing dishes is not just a chore; it's a way to contribute to your household and the planet. Also, by using these eco-friendly and efficient techniques, you're getting your dishes clean and caring for our environment. So, roll up your sleeves, and let's make those dishes shine sustainably!

HANDLING HOUSEHOLD TASKS

Now, let's turn our attention to some handy skills that can make you feel like a true problem-solver at home. I remember when Aysel was learning to change batteries for our winter ornaments. With a small screwdriver in hand, she carefully opened the battery compartment, replaced the old batteries with new ones, and was delighted to see the ornaments light up again! Changing batteries and handling basic maintenance tasks are small but mighty ways to contribute to your household. Let's get our hands a little technical!

CHANGING BATTERIES

1. Identify Battery Type: First, find out what batteries you need. Is it AA, AAA, or something else? Check the device for clues.
2. Safe Removal: Open the battery compartment, usually on the back of the device. Remove the old batteries and notice how they're placed; this is how the new ones should go in.
3. Insert New Batteries: Put in the new batteries, matching the + (positive) and - (negative) ends correctly. Most devices have a little diagram showing which way the batteries should face.
4. Close and Test: Close the battery compartment and test the device to make sure it's working.
5. Rechargeable Batteries: Look for batteries that can be recharged and avoid those that are one-use-only.

Battery Safety Tip: Always dispose of old batteries properly. Don't mix old and new batteries in the same device, as this can affect performance and safety.

UNCLOGGING DRAINS

- Safety First: Never use your hands to clear a drain. Always use tools like a plunger or a plumber's snake.

- Plunging: If it's a minor clog, try using a plunger. Cover the drain with the plunger, pump it several times, then pull it off. This often clears things up.
- Baking Soda and Vinegar: For a non-chemical approach, pour baking soda (a coup would be enough) down the drain, followed by a cup of vinegar. Wait and then flush.

WATERING AND CARING FOR HOUSEPLANTS

Houseplants aren't just decorative; they can purify the air and improve your environment.

1. Check Soil Moisture: Check if the soil is dry a couple of inches down before watering—only water when necessary to avoid overwatering, which can harm plants.
2. Watering Technique: Use a watering can or cup. Water the soil directly, not the leaves, until water drains from the bottom.
3. Understanding Light: Different plants require varying amounts of light. Some grow under direct sunlight, but others prefer indirect light.
4. Regular Care: Encourage a routine of checking the plants once a week for watering needs, trimming dead leaves, and ensuring they get enough light.

PLANT CARE ACTIVITY!

Start a diary to track when you water your plants and note any new growth. It's fun to see your plants thrive and remember their care schedule.

Environmental Tip: To be eco-friendly, use leftover water from glasses or bottles to water your plants. It's a small step toward ecological conservation.

BASICS OF USING TOOLS

Great! Now, let's get a bit more hands-on and talk about using essential tools. Knowing how to use a hammer, a screwdriver, and even an adjustable wrench can be handy for various tasks around the house and outdoors. I remember when Shani used a hammer for the first time. She was helping to fix a loose board on our garden fence. With some guidance, she gently tapped the nail and then drove it in confidently; a proud moment for her! Let's nail these skills down!

USING HAMMER

1. Safety First: Always wear protective eyewear when using a hammer.
2. Proper Grip: Hold near the end of the handle for balance and power.
3. Aim and Tap: Gently tap the nail to start it in the wood, then swing in a controlled motion.
4. Straight Hits: Aim for straight, direct hits to drive the nail in without bending it.

Real-Life Scenario: Imagine you're helping to build a small bookshelf. Using a hammer to fasten the nails securely is a crucial step in this project.

USING A SCREWDRIVER

1. Select the Right Type: There are two main types of screwdrivers: flathead and Phillips. Match the screwdriver to the kind of screw you're working with.
2. Firm Grip: Hold the handle firmly with one hand while guiding the tip into the screw head with the other.
3. Turn Right to Tighten: Remember the saying, 'Righty tighty, lefty loosey.' Turn the screwdriver clockwise to tighten a screw and counterclockwise to loosen it.
4. Steady Pressure: Apply constant pressure while turning the screwdriver to keep the tip from slipping out of the screw head.

Real-Life Scenario: A perfect time to use a screwdriver is when assembling a simple chair or fixing a loose doorknob.

USING AN ADJUSTABLE WRENCH

1. Identify the Nut or Bolt: First, find the nut or bolt you need to work on.
2. Adjust the Wrench: Open the jaws of the wrench by turning the screw near the handle. Adjust it until the jaws fit snugly around the nut or bolt.
3. Grip and Turn: Hold the wrench firmly and turn it in your desired direction.

4. Steady Pressure: Apply constant pressure and turn the wrench.
5. Re-adjust if Needed: If the wrench gets loose, stop and readjust it for a tighter fit.

Real-Life Scenario: Use an adjustable wrench when you're putting together a bicycle or tightening a leaky faucet.

USING NEEDLE-NOSE PLIERS

1. Grip the Object: Open the pliers by pressing the handles and use the long, thin tips to grip small objects or to reach into tight spaces.
2. Apply Pressure: Gently squeeze the handles to grip the object firmly but without too much force to avoid damaging it.
3. Twist or Bend: Use the pliers to twist wires or bend small metal pieces. Always be gentle and precise.
4. Release Gently: Once done, release the pressure and carefully remove the pliers.

Real-Life Scenario: Use needle-nose pliers when threading a needle in a tight space or manipulating small components in electronics repair, such as bending wires.

USING A GARDEN TROWEL

1. Hold Correctly: Grip the trowel's handle firmly with your dominant hand.
2. Digging: Press the trowel's blade into the soil and use a lever motion to lift or turn the soil. This is great for making holes for planting.
3. Planting: Place your plant or seeds into the prepared hole. Use the trowel to cover the roots or seeds gently with soil.
4. Smoothing Soil: Use the flat side of the trowel to pat down the soil gently around the plant.

Real-Life Scenario: Use a garden trowel when planting flowers in your garden or adding herbs to a small kitchen garden.

SIMPLE PROJECT: PICTURE FRAME STAND

To put your new skills to the test, why not try making a simple picture frame stand? You'll need a small wooden plank, a few nails, and your trusty hammer. Measure and mark where you want the nails to go, then carefully hammer them in to create a stand at the back of the frame. It's an easy yet satisfying project to start with!

Getting comfortable with these tools is not only super helpful but also really empowering. Whether you're hanging a picture, tightening a loose screw, or finding your way in the woods, these are skills that will come in handy throughout life. Remember, when using any tool, safety comes first! Always use tools under adult supervision. It's not just about getting the job done; it's about learning and having fun along the way!

Keeping Spaces Tidy

It's time to talk about organizing! Keeping your space tidy is not just about cleaning; it's about creating a happy and calm environment where you can find things easily and feel great. Here are some simple tips to keep your spaces wonderfully organized:

DECLUTTERING

- Sort Your Stuff: First, go through your things and decide what you need and what you can give away or recycle. A simple rule is if you haven't used it in a year, you probably don't need it.
- Categorize: Organize your items into categories: clothes, books, toys, etc. It's easier to decide where things should go when they're sorted.

Aysel and Shani's Room: Aysel and Shani share a room with a bunk bed. They had to get creative about using their space efficiently. They started by sorting through their toys and clothes, deciding to donate the ones they no longer use.

CREATING A PLACE FOR EVERYTHING

- Designate Spaces: Decide where each category of items will live. Books on the shelf, toys in the toy box, clothes in the closet, and so on.
- Use Storage Solutions: Bins, baskets, and boxes can be lifesavers. Label them for easy identification. Repurpose old containers for storage (like using an old mug to hold pens).
- Space-Saving Tip: You can use vertical space by adding shelves for your books and toys. Under-bed storage boxes are perfect for out-of-season clothes.

REGULAR CLEANING AND TIDYING

- Make a Schedule: Set a regular weekly time for tidying your room. This could be a quick daily tidy-up and a more thorough clean once a week.
- Put Things Back: After using something, return it where it belongs. This simple habit makes a huge difference.

Décor and Personal Touch

- Your Style: Decorate your space in a way that makes you happy. Whether it's posters, your artwork, or fun pillows, make it yours!
- DIY Organizing Projects: Get creative with DIY (Do It Yourself) projects for organizing, like decorating your storage boxes or creating a fun jewelry holder.

A Fun Game: Organize it!

- Objective: To categorize items in the room as quickly as possible.
- How to Play: Set a timer for 10 minutes. Pick up items and decide whether they will be kept, donated, or thrown away. The goal is to sort as many items as possible before the timer goes off.
- Variation for Siblings: If you share your room, like Aysel and Shani, compete to see who can sort their items faster.

Remember, organizing is about making your space work for you. It's not about perfection; it's about creating a place where you feel comfortable and happy. So, let's roll up our sleeves and get organized!

Simple Sewing

Next up is sewing! Don't worry; it's not as complicated as it might seem. Sewing is a super helpful skill, whether fixing a loose button or mending a small tear in your favorite dress. Let's get started with some basic sewing techniques:

Getting Your Sewing Kit Ready

- Essential Supplies: For basic sewing, you'll need needles, thread, scissors, and spare buttons. You can find these in a simple sewing kit.
- Thread Choices: Choose a thread color that matches your fabric. This makes your sewing less noticeable.

Threading the Needle

- Cutting the Thread: Cut a thread length, not too long, or it might tangle. About 18 inches is a good start.

- Threading: Lick the end of the thread (to make it easier to handle) and carefully push it through the eye of the needle. Then, tie a small knot at the other end.

BASIC STITCH (RUNNING STITCH)

1. Starting: Push the needle up from the back of the fabric so the knot stops at the back.
2. The Stitch: Make tiny stitches in and out of the fabric, going forward each time. Try to keep your stitches even.
3. Securing the End: Once you've finished your line of stitches, make a small stitch on the back and loop the thread through it to make a knot.

SEWING ON A BUTTON

1. Positioning the Button: Place the button where it needs to go. If there's an old threadmark, use that as your guide.
2. Starting the Thread: Start from the back of the fabric, bringing the needle up through one of the buttonholes.
3. Attaching the Button: Stitch up from the bottom and down from the top, alternating holes until the button is secure.
4. Finishing Off: Finish with the needle on the back of the fabric, tie a knot, and cut off any excess thread.

MENDING A TEAR

1. Align the Fabric: Line up the torn edges so they're even.
2. Sewing the Tear: Use a running stitch to bring the edges together, making the stitches small gently so they're less visible.
3. Finishing Up: Secure the end with a knot and trim the excess thread.

SEWING TIPS AND SUSTAINABILITY

- Use a thimble to protect your fingers, especially when handling tough fabrics.
- Repurpose fabric scraps or old clothing for buttons, patches, or practice materials. It's a great way to be sustainable and creative!

SIMPLE SEWING PROJECT: DECORATE A CLOTH BAG

Materials: A plain cloth bag, various colored threads, needles, and any decorations you'd like (fabric scraps, buttons, etc.).

Project: Use your basic stitches to decorate your bag. You can create designs with different colored threads, sew on patches made from fabric scraps, or add buttons for a fun look.

Sewing is a bit like art; it takes practice, but you can fix so many things once you get the hang of it. Don't be discouraged if your first few stitches aren't perfect or if you find threading the needle tricky.

Every stitch you make is progress, and soon, you'll be able to handle more complex sewing tasks. So, keep practicing, be creative, and, most importantly, have fun!

WRAP-UP

As we wrap up this first chapter on Basic Survival and Home Skills, remember that each skill you've learned here, be it sewing, cooking, or organizing, is a step towards becoming more independent and resourceful. These aren't just chores but opportunities to grow and express yourself. Embrace these lessons, experiment with them, and enjoy your journey of learning and discovery!

CHAPTER TWO

MONEY MATTERS SKILLS

Welcome to Chapter 2, Money Matters Skills, a crucial adventure into the world of money management! You might think managing money is just for adults, but it's actually a superpower you can start developing right now. From learning how to save your allowance for that special toy to understanding how chores can turn into earnings, we will explore all the fun and important aspects of handling money. Have you ever saved up for something you really wanted? Well, get ready to become even more thoughtful about saving, spending, and making your money work for you. We'll dive into easy budgeting tips, creative ways to earn and save, and even start unraveling the mysteries of banks and accounts. So, let's turn the page and begin our journey to becoming young money management experts!

MONEY SMART

Let's talk about what money is. It's not just coins; it's a tool we use to exchange for things we need, like food and clothes, and things we love, like books and games. Understanding the value of money helps us make smart decisions on how to use it.

EARNING YOUR OWN MONEY

Earning money can be a great adventure! Aysel and Shani began understanding this when they started small jobs around the house. They've planned things like dog walking to earn money and save it for what they want. They felt proud and excited to earn their own money, and you can, too. Whether it's pet sitting, babysitting, or making and selling crafts, every penny you earn is a reward for your effort and creativity.

THE POWER OF SAVING

Saving money is like a magical process where your small savings grow over time into something big and exciting. Aysel and Shani have their own savings jars, and they love watching their savings increase. They're learning patience and the importance of planning for bigger things they want in the future. Whether it's a special toy, a book, or something even more significant, watching your savings grow is both fun and rewarding.

SPENDING SMARTLY

It is great when you see your savings grow. It's about watching your small efforts bloom into something extraordinary. However, saving isn't just about setting money aside; it's about making intelligent choices when you need to buy things and decide what you truly value.

BUDGETING: YOUR MONEY MAP

A budget helps you see the big picture and make smart choices with your money. Write in a journal the things you want to buy and their price, sum up and see how much money you need. Compare with the amount you have. Establish an amount you are going to spend. That is your budget. Then erase those things you do not need/want right now until you get to the amount of your budget.

GIVING AND SHARING

Money isn't just for spending on ourselves; it's also for helping others. I want to share with you a touching story about Aysel and Shani. They once learned about children suffering in war-affected areas. Wanting to help, they decided to start a donation campaign. To kickstart their initiative, they donated a part of their own savings to invite others to join. Their small but significant contribution inspired our family and friends to contribute. Together, we collected funds for these children.

Sharing what we have with others is one of the most heartwarming aspects of handling money. This experience was a profound lesson for all of us about the power and importance of giving and sharing. It reminds us that we can all be part of positive change, regardless of age.

So, are you ready to join on this adventure to become money-smart? Let's learn about making choices that not only benefit us but also make the world a little brighter!

DREAM CHASING

It is time to learn one thing that will help us forever: setting and achieving personal goals! Whether it's saving up for something special or accomplishing a new skill, learning to set and achieve goals is like having a secret map to your dreams. And guess what? You're the captain of this adventure!

GOAL SETTING

Setting a goal starts with an idea or a dream. Maybe you want to learn a new skill, save up for something special, or get better at a hobby. The key is to choose something that excites you and feels important.

When setting your goal, make it clear and achievable. For instance, saying, "I want to read more," is a bit vague. Instead, try "I want to read one new book monthly." This gives you a specific goal to aim for. Let me share the steps I follow all the time I need to set a goal:

1. Identify Your Interest: Start by thinking about what you really enjoy or are curious about. It could be anything from learning a new language, getting better at a sport, or even starting a small garden.
2. Make it Specific: Once you have an idea, shape it into a specific goal. Instead of saying, "I want to save money," say, "I want to save $50 for a new book series I love."
3. Set a Deadline: Having a timeline makes your goal more concrete. Decide when you want to achieve your goal. It could be in a few weeks, months, or by the end of the school year.

PLANNING YOUR STEPS

After setting your goal, the next step is to plan how to achieve it. Here's how you can do that:

1. Break it: Divide your goal into smaller tasks. If your goal is to learn a new dance, your steps could be: find a tutorial, practice the first set of moves, then the next, and so on. If you want to save $50, think about how much you need to keep each week and how you'll do it.
2. Create a Schedule: Allocate specific weekly times to work on your goal. If you're learning to play an instrument, you might set aside 30 minutes daily for practice.
3. Track Your Progress: Keep a journal or a chart to mark your progress. This will help you see how far you've come and what you need to focus on next.
4. Stay Committed: Some days will be more challenging than others. Remember why you set your goal and keep going.
5. Celebrate: When you reach your goal, celebrate! You've earned it.

These steps are like a ladder leading you to your goal. If your goal is to read more books, your steps could include choosing the books you want to read, setting aside time each day for reading, and tracking your progress.

Reflect and Adjust

As you work towards your goal, it's okay to adjust your plan; maybe you find out you need more time or different resources. It's all part of the learning process.

Let me share a story about Aysel and Shani that perfectly illustrates goal setting and fulfillment. For their birthday, they both decided they wanted to learn to play the ukulele. But instead of asking for it as a gift, they set it as their goal to buy their ukuleles. They started saving a part of their weekly allowance and the money they received as gifts. Staying focused despite temptations to spend elsewhere, they eventually kept enough. The joy and pride they felt upon buying their ukuleles were immense, teaching them the value of patience, saving, and fulfilling a goal they had set for themselves.

Chore Cash: Turning Tasks into Treasure

Now, let's talk about a fun and rewarding part of being responsible: earning your own money! You might wonder, "How can I, as a kid, earn money?" Well, you'll be surprised at how many opportunities are around you; from dog walking to organizing a garage sale, each chore you do can be a stepping stone to your financial independence, even at a young age. Let me show you some cool and creative ways you can start earning:

1. Dog Walking:

- Perfect for pet lovers! If you're around 10-12 years old, this can be a great fit. For those younger, consider being a pet care assistant (helping with feeding or playing under adult supervision). Always walk dogs in familiar, safe neighborhoods; starting with manageable, smaller dogs is best.

2. Babysitting:

- This is more suitable for the older girls in our age range, like 11-12. If you're younger, start by assisting an older sibling or family member with babysitting. Always babysit in a known environment and have an adult nearby whom you can call for help. Ensure you know the basics of child care and always have emergency contact information handy.

3. Cookie Selling or Lemonade Stand:

- This is great for all ages! Younger kids should have an adult help with the baking or setting up the stand (or you can try our non-bake cookies recipe included in Chapter One!) Learn about handling money and customer service, but always set up your stand in a safe area where an adult can keep an eye on things.

4. Car Washing:

- Ideal for those older and stronger, maybe around 11-12 years old. Handling the hose and buckets can be challenging for younger kids. Ensure an adult is around to supervise, especially when working near the road.

5. Lawn Mowing:

- This is best for the oldest in our group, around 12 years old, and always with adult supervision. Lawnmowers can be dangerous, so it's essential that an adult is present and that you've been taught how to use the mower safely.

6. Tutoring Younger Kids:

- If you excel in a subject and enjoy teaching, this can be appropriate for all ages in our range. But make sure an adult is around if you need help, especially when meeting new families.

7. Organizing Garage Sales:

- This is something the whole family can get involved in. Younger children can help with setting up and managing a small sale of their own under the watchful eye of an adult.

8. Crafts for Sale:

- Perfect for all ages! For the creatively inclined, making and selling crafts like friendship bracelets or homemade cards is a fun way to earn. Set up a small booth or sell to friends and family.

9. Storytime Helper:

- If you love reading and storytelling, consider as a story-time helper at local libraries or family gatherings. It's a wonderful way to spread the joy of reading.

SAFETY AND PERMISSIONS

- Very important: with all these activities, your safety is the most valuable thing. Always talk to your parents before starting any of these chores. Get their permission and ask for their help if you need it. Some tasks require constant adult supervision; for others, it is enough to let an adult know what you're doing.
- Earning money through chores is not only about making some extra cash; it's about learning valuable life skills. But it's crucial to choose appropriate chores for your age and always have your parents or an adult's guidance to ensure your safety. So, choose wisely, have fun, and learn the ropes of responsibility and independence!

MARKET MAGIC: SELLING YOUR SKILLS AND CREATIONS

After learning about different chores, you can do to earn money, you might wonder, "Well, yes, but how will people know about my services?" This is where "Market Magic" comes into play! It's all about finding creative ways to let people know about your terrific services or products.

Marketing is like sharing a secret that you're excited about. It's about telling a story that interests people in what you have to offer. Say you're offering to walk dogs, or you've baked some delicious cookies to sell. The way you share this with others can really spark their interest.

- Understand Your Offering: Know precisely what you're providing. If you're selling cookies, what makes them unique? Maybe they're the chewiest, creamier cookies ever. Knowing this makes it easier to explain why others should try them.
- Who Wants to Know? Think about who would be interested in your service. For dog walking, your audience might be busy neighbors. If you have a lemonade stand, it might be people looking for a cool drink on a sunny day.
- Make Eye-Catching Flyers: Use bright colors and clear words on posters or flyers. You can make super cute flyers for your bake sale, with pictures of their treats and a fun message.
- Spread the Word: The best marketing can be just talking about what you're doing. Tell your friends who can tell their parents, and so on. It's like a chain reaction of excitement!
- Confidence and Friendliness: When you talk about what you're offering, be confident and friendly. If you believe in your product or service, others will, too.
- Provide Great Service: Keep your customers happy! Excellent service means they might tell others about you or return for more. Always smile and thank your customers, and you'll leave a lasting impression.

Marketing isn't just about selling; it's about sharing something you're passionate about. It's a great way to express creativity and connect with your community. So, put on your thinking cap and start spreading the word.

YOUR GUIDE TO OPENING YOUR FIRST ACCOUNT

Alright, it's time to talk about something really cool: opening your first bank account. This isn't just about stashing your cash; it's about stepping into a new level of independence and boosting your confidence. While the age for starting a bank account varies, usually, by the time you're 10 to 12, you're ready to dive in.

- Why It's Awesome: Think of a bank account as your personal treasure chest that teaches you super-important stuff about money. It's not just about saving; it's about getting wise with your finances. And guess what? It feels pretty grown-up, too!

- Choosing a Bank: There are many banks out there with accounts just for kids and teens. You and your folks can have a mini-adventure comparing them. Look for one that's friendly to young savers like you.
- Getting Ready: You'll need an ID (like your birth certificate). Your mom or dad will need their ID, too. It's like a mini-mission to gather all the proper documents.
- Bank Visit: Visiting a bank feels super official, right? It's an adventure in itself. You'll learn a lot about how banks work and what it means to have an account.
- The Rules: Every country has its own rules for young bankers. Make sure you know the ins and outs of your account. It's like learning the rules of a new game.
- Saving Up: Once your account's all set, the real fun begins: saving! Watching your money grow is like watching a plant you've watered flourish. Even saving a little bit regularly can lead to a big reward.

So, getting your bank account is more than saving money; it's about taking a giant leap toward independence and learning some serious life skills. Are you ready for this exciting journey? I bet you are!

SMART GROCERY SHOPPING TIPS

Now, let's dive into a super important skill: grocery shopping on a budget. It might sound like something only grown-ups do, but trust me, it's never too early to learn how to shop smartly. Plus, it can be pretty fun! Here are some easy tips to help you become a savvy shopper:

PLANNING IS KEY

- Make a List: Before heading to the store, list what you need. This helps you avoid buying things you don't really need.
- Plan Your Meals: Think about what meals you'd like for the week. This helps buy only what's necessary, reduce waste, and save money.

UNDERSTANDING BUDGET

- Set a Budget: Decide how much money you can spend on groceries. Stick to this amount to learn about spending within limits.
- Compare Prices: Look at different brands and compare prices. Sometimes, store brands are cheaper and just as good as name brands.

Shopping Smartly

- Use Coupons and Deals: Look out for coupons in newspapers or online. Stores also have deals; keep an eye on those!
- Buy in Bulk: Sometimes, buying wholesale can save money, especially for non-perishable items like rice or pasta.
- Seasonal Shopping: Buying fruits and vegetables in their season is usually cheaper (and they taste better, too!).

Avoid Impulse Buys

- Stick to Your List: Avoid being tempted by things that aren't on your list, especially at the checkout area.
- Don't Shop Hungry: Everything looks tempting when you're hungry, leading to unnecessary purchases.

Learning the Store Layout

- Familiarize Yourself with the Store: Knowing where everything is can save time and help you make better choices.

Check Out and Beyond

- Self-Checkout: If the store has a self-checkout, try it out. It's a great way to learn about handling money and transactions.
- Review Your Purchase: After shopping, review your receipt to understand where your money went. This can help you plan better for next time.

Grocery shopping is a fantastic way to learn about budgeting, nutrition, and making independent choices. It's also an excellent opportunity to help out your family and contribute to planning meals. So next time you go grocery shopping, remember these tips and see how much fun and educational it can be!

PROBLEM-SOLVING AND DECISION MAKING

Life is full of little puzzles and decisions, and learning how to tackle them is a super important skill.

1. **Problem-solving is like being a detective:** you look at the clues (the problem details) and try to find the best solution. And decision-making? It's about choosing the best option from what's available. Let me show you how to get good at both.
2. **Understand the Problem:** First, you need to understand what the problem is. Ask yourself: What exactly is going wrong? For instance, if you and your sister both want to use the same art supplies at the same time, the problem is sharing resources.
3. **Think of Possible Solutions:** Next, brainstorm different ways to solve the problem. With the art supplies, one solution could be creating a schedule so you both get equal time.
4. **Evaluate the Solutions:** Look at your solutions and think about their pros and cons. Which solution is fair and makes everyone mostly happy? Sometimes, there's no perfect answer, but there's usually one that works best.
5. **Make a Decision:** Once you've thought it through, it's time to decide. Choose the solution that seems best and go with it. Remember, making a decision is better than not making one at all.
6. **Put Your Decision into Action:** Now, it's time to try out your solution. This is where you see if your idea works in real life.
7. **Review and Adjust:** After trying your solution, think about how it went. Did it solve the problem? If not, it's okay! You can always try a different solution. It's all about learning and adjusting.

For instance, Aysel and Shani once disagreed about who should get to play with their new puzzle game first. They each presented their case, thought about fair ways to share, and decided to take turns, setting a timer to ensure each had an equal chance. This way, they solved the problem and learned a valuable lesson in sharing and fairness.

In life, you'll face many decisions and problems, but with these steps, you'll have a roadmap to find solutions. It is important to remember every problem you solve makes you smarter, and every decision you make makes you stronger. So, face those challenges head-on; you've got this!

ORGANIZING AND PRIORITIZING TASKS

This is all about organizing your day to get things done and still have time for fun! Imagine your day as a big, colorful puzzle. Each task you have (like school, homework, or playing) is a piece of the puzzle. The challenge is to fit all these pieces together in a fun and balanced way.

Let's start with a to-do list. This is like drawing a map for your day. You can list everything you need to do, like homework or chores, and the fun stuff you want to do, like playing or reading.

All tasks are important, but some are like sparkly gems that must be done first. For example, finishing up schoolwork is more important than organizing your toy shelf. Learning to pick out these 'sparkly gem' tasks is a big part of managing your time.

A secret tip is setting time limits. Ever start playing a game, and then, whoosh, where did the time go? Setting a timer helps you keep track, giving you time for all the fun and essential stuff.

Balance is key! After you finish a big task, reward yourself with something you love to do. This keeps you happy and ready for the next adventure.

Sometimes, things don't go as planned, and that's okay! Being flexible and changing your plan is a super important part of managing your time. At the end of each day, take a moment to reflect. Did you manage to do everything on your list? If not, think about what you can do differently tomorrow. This is how you get better at managing your time. So, let's get our time management capes on and make every day a fantastic adventure!

Wrap-up

Whew! What a journey we've had in Chapter Two! From becoming savvy with money management to mastering the art of time management and even dreaming up big goals for the future. Remember, every skill we've discussed here, whether making intelligent choices with your allowance or learning the ropes of opening a bank account, is like adding a superpower to your toolkit for life.

These skills aren't just about managing money or time; they're about building confidence and independence and stepping boldly into new adventures. I hope these lessons equip you with valuable life skills and inspire you to pursue your dreams confidently and continuously. Remember, every step you take in learning and growing today shapes the strong, independent, and empowered women you are becoming. So, let's keep this adventure going and turn the page to see what exciting things await us in Chapter Three!

CHAPTER THREE

GEMS: GIRLS IN ENGINEERING, MATH, AND SCIENCE

Hello girls! Here, we will embark on an exciting exploration of the world of GEMS (Girls in Engineering, Math, and Science). We will break some myths and show that these fields are for everyone, including Aysel, Shani, and, of course, you! We'll start with the magic of coding and programming, where you'll learn how to create and communicate with computers in a fun and creative way. Then, we'll dive into some cool engineering projects you can do with your hands, building models and simple machines that bring engineering concepts. And let's not forget about math; it's all around us in daily life, and we'll discover just how practical and exciting it can be. So, gear up for some GEMS-tastic adventures that will boost your confidence and show you how these skills can open doors to a world of possibilities!

EVERYDAY SCIENCE EXPERIMENTS

DANCING MILK EXPERIMENT:

- **Materials:** Milk, food coloring, dish soap, cotton swabs, shallow dish.
- **Steps:** Pour milk into the dish. Add drops of different food coloring. Using a cotton swab, dip it in dish soap and touch the center of the milk.
- *Science Concept:* The soap reduces the milk's surface tension, causing the colors to swirl and dance. This demonstrates how detergents break down fats, similar to how dish soap cleans greasy dishes.

Magic Water and Paper Trick:

- **Materials:** Glass, water, cardstock paper.
- **Steps:** Fill the glass with water. Place the paper over the glass mouth. Turn the glass upside down, holding the paper with your hand. Carefully remove your hand.
- *Science Concept:* Air pressure keeps the paper in place, preventing water from spilling. This principle is behind weather patterns and how airplanes fly.

Volcano Experiment:

- **Materials:** Baking soda, vinegar, food coloring, container.
- **Steps:** Mix baking soda and food coloring in a container. Pour vinegar over it.
- *Science Concept:* The reaction between baking soda (base) and vinegar (acid) creates carbon dioxide gas, simulating volcanic eruptions.

Floating Egg Experiment:

- **Materials:** Two eggs, two glasses of water, salt.
- **Steps:** Fill one glass with plain water and another with salt water. Gently place an egg in each glass.
- *Science Concept:* The egg floats in saltwater due to increased density. This demonstrates buoyancy, a principle that explains why ships float and how submarines control depth.

Code Quest: Discovering the Fun of Programming

Now, let's dive into the fascinating world of Basic Coding and Programming! You might wonder why we should learn to code. Try to imagine coding as a unique language that lets us communicate with computers, creating everything from games, apps, and even robots! In this section, we'll start with the basics and gradually build up to creating your programs. Whether it's making a simple game or designing an interactive story, you'll discover how coding is helpful, incredibly fun, and creative. Are you ready to unlock the magic of coding and see where your imagination takes you?

When we code, we're not just playing with computers; we're learning to think in new and creative ways. Coding helps us solve problems, design beautiful things, and understand how the technology around us works. It's like having the key to a secret world where anything is possible. And the best part? Coding is for everyone! So, let's start this adventure and see what amazing things we can create with code!

UNDERSTANDING THE BASICS CODING CONCEPTS.

There are some basic coding concepts that are the building blocks of this digital magic. We'll start with 'Code' itself and then dive into fun concepts like algorithms, loops, variables, and more. Each concept is a crucial piece of the puzzle in understanding how to communicate with computers.

- **Code:** Code is the language we use to talk to computers. It's like giving instructions to a friend on how to do something. When we write code, we are telling the computer exactly what we want it to do, step by step. Just like we use words to communicate, computers use code to understand and carry out tasks.
- **HTML. The Skeleton of Websites:** HyperText Markup Language (HTML) is like the skeleton of a website. Explain it as a simple way of creating and organizing content on the web. You can compare it to building a house, where HTML forms the structure: walls, floors, and ceilings.
- **CSS. Adding Style to Websites:** CSS, or Cascading Style Sheets, gives websites their unique look. It's like the paint, decorations, and style of a house built with HTML. Introduce CSS as a tool to make websites more visually appealing by changing colors, fonts, and layouts.
- **Binary:** The Language of Computers: Binary is the most basic language of computers, using only '1s' and '0s'. It's like the alphabet for computers.
- **Algorithms:** Think of an algorithm as a recipe for your computer. It's a step-by-step guide telling it what to do. Like following a recipe to bake a chocolate cake, computers follow algorithms to complete tasks.
- **Loops:** Loops are like the magic trick of coding. They let you repeat a task over and over without writing the same instructions again and again. Imagine wanting to draw ten stars. Instead of writing 'draw a star' 10 times, you just tell the computer to 'draw a star' in a loop ten times!

41

- **Variables:** Variables are like special boxes where you can store things in a code. You might have a box labeled 'Age' where you keep your age. Whenever you need to use your age in the code, you just open the 'Age' box, and there it is!
- **Conditional Statements:** These are the 'if-then' choices in coding. For example, if it's raining, then take an umbrella. In coding, these statements help the computer make decisions based on different situations.
- **Debugging:** Even the best coders make mistakes, and that's where debugging comes in. It's like being a detective, finding and fixing errors in your code. Remember, finding a bug is a chance to learn and improve your coding skills!

EXPLORING KID-FRIENDLY CODING PLATFORMS

Alright, let me share some fantastic coding platforms designed just for you. Think of these as a kind of digital playground where you can learn coding in a super fun way!

- **Hopscotch:** This is a place where you can let your imagination run wild! You'll find Hopscotch perfect if you're between 8 and 12 years old. It's similar to a digital canvas where you can create your own games and animations. The best part? It's free to download! You can get some extra cool features with in-app purchases, but you can do loads without them. Remember, you might need your parent's permission to download the app and make any purchases.
- **Imagilabs:** This one is super cool, especially if you love mixing coding with creativity. Imagilabs is all about making coding a part of the real world. You can use their app to code things for a smart accessory: imagine coding your designs that light up! While the app is free, you might need to get a special accessory to see your code come to life. Parental guidance is recommended, especially when considering the purchase of their accessory.
- **Erase All Kittens (EAK):** If you ever dreamt of being a web designer or game creator, you'll love this! EAK is a bit different because you get to learn HTML and CSS! the real stuff websites are made of. It's a subscription-based platform, but it's worth it because you'll be creating your very own web pages and games in no time. Since this involves an online subscription, make sure to have your parent's permission and supervision.
- **Create & Learn:** This is about making learning fun and engaging. It offers a variety of live online classes in coding taught by expert instructors. The courses cover different topics and coding languages, which is perfect for diving deeper into coding. While some introductory classes are free, more advanced courses are paid, providing a structured

learning path with personalized feedback. As these are live, online sessions, it is very important to have your parents' permission.

In addition to these fantastic digital platforms, there are also 'unplugged' options for learning coding concepts without a computer. These activities are perfect for times when you want to step away from the screen but still indulge in the fun of coding.

UNPLUGGED ACTIVITY

Binary Bracelets: This activity involves creating bracelets using binary code, the language that computers use to communicate. It's a crafty and creative way to learn how computers store and process information. Here you have the steps:

1. **Choose a Word:** Select a word or initials.
2. **Find Binary Codes:** Use the chart to find the 5-bit binary code for each letter in your word.

Letter	5-Bit Binary	Letter	5-Bit Binary
A	00001	N	1110
B	00010	O	1111
C	00011	P	10000
D	00100	Q	10001
E	00101	R	10010
F	00110	S	10011
G	00111	T	10100
H	01000	U	10101
I	01001	V	10110
J	01010	W	10111
K	01011	X	11000
L	01100	Y	11001
M	01101	Z	11010

3. **Select Bead Colors:** Decide on two colors of beads, one for 0 and another for 1.
4. **String the Beads:** Following the binary code for each letter, string the beads onto your bracelet.

43

Map Navigator: We will play with something called "pseudo-code." It's like a secret language telling computers (or even your friends) exactly how to solve fun puzzles and find hidden treasures. Let's dive into some awesome pseudo-code adventures!

- **Objective:** Help your friend find the hidden treasure on a map using pseudo-code.
- **Materials:**

  o A simple map (you can draw one or print it). Include landmarks like trees, a pond, a bridge, etc.
  o A small toy or sticker to be the 'treasure.'

- **Steps:**

  o Place the Treasure: Put your toy or sticker on a secret spot on the map.
  o Write the Pseudo-Code: Give your friend written instructions to find the treasure. Use simple commands like 'walk to the tree,' 'turn left,' 'move forward ten steps,' etc.

- **Test it Out:** Your friend follows your pseudo-code to find the treasure. If they can't find it, check your instructions and try again!

```css
Start at the big rock.
Move forward 5 steps.
Turn right and walk to the tree.
Turn left and take 8 steps.
Look down for the treasure!
```

These unplugged activities are not only educational but also fun; they provide a hands-on approach to understanding coding and computer science basics.

These platforms aren't just for learning; they're for having fun, being creative, and showing the world what you can do. It's important to remember that while these platforms are fantastic for learning and exploring, it's always best to involve your parents or guardians; they can help you set up accounts safely, choose the right courses, and ensure that you're learning in a secure environment. With these tools, you're not just playing but preparing for a world full of exciting possibilities. So, let's get coding and see what amazing things you can create!

Have you ever wondered how coding touches almost every part of our lives? Let's explore the fantastic ways coding is used in various fields and how it's making a big difference!

- **Environment:** Coding isn't just about screens and keyboards; it's about our planet, too! Women coders are at the forefront of developing apps that monitor climate change, track wildlife, and help reduce pollution. They use code to analyze data and develop solutions to protect our environment.
- **Healthcare:** Coders are like the health heroes of technology. They create apps and software that help doctors diagnose diseases, track patient health, and even perform surgeries with robotic arms. For instance, female coders like Reshma Saujani, founder of Girls Who Code, inspire more girls to enter this field and innovate in healthcare.
- **Space Exploration:** Imagine coding a robot to explore Mars or a satellite to study distant galaxies. Women in coding are playing a crucial role in space agencies like NASA, writing code that sends rockets into space and analyzes data from other planets.
- **Art and Music:** Did you know coding can be artistic? Female coders blend technology with art to create digital masterpieces and compose electronic music. They show us that coding is not just about logic; it's about imagination and creativity, too.
- **Entertainment:** From movies to video games, coding is the magic behind the scenes. Female game developers and animators use coding to create stunning visual effects or characters. It's like turning a creative idea into an exciting reality!
- **Everyday Gadgets:** The smartphone you use, the smartwatch on your wrist, or even the car your family drives, coders make these intelligent and valuable. Women in tech design apps and software that make our gadgets fun and functional.

Coding isn't just for computers; it's a tool that's shaping our world in incredible ways. And the best part? Girls like you are leading this change!

By learning to code, you're playing with technology, and also you're becoming a creator who can positively impact many fields. Who knows, maybe one day, your coding skills will lead to a fantastic discovery or invention!

SIMPLE ENGINEERING PROJECTS

Are you ready to get your hands a little busy and your brain buzzing with excitement? Engineering isn't just about big machines and buildings; it's about creating, inventing, and solving problems. Here, you have three fun projects you can do at home to discover the joy of engineering!

BUILD A MINI CATAPULT:

- **Materials:** 7 popsicle sticks, four rubber bands, a plastic spoon, and a small pom-pom or cotton ball.
- **Steps:**

  1. Stack 5 popsicle sticks and bind them with two rubber bands at each end.
  2. Take the remaining two popsicle sticks and attach them at one end with another rubber band, creating a V shape.
  3. Slide the stack of 5 sticks between the 2 in the V shape. Use the last rubber band to attach the spoon to the top stick of the V.
  4. Place your pom-pom in the spoon, press down, and let go! Watch your catapult launch the pom-pom!

SIMPLE WIND-POWERED CAR:

- **Materials:** Cardboard, two straws, four bottle caps, a wooden skewer, tape, scissors, and a small balloon.
- **Steps:**

  1. Cut a rectangular piece of cardboard; this will be your car's body.
  2. Make holes in the center of each bottle cap. These will be your wheels.
  3. Cut the wooden skewer into two pieces. Slide them through the straws and attach the bottle cap wheels.
  4. Attach the straws with wheels to the underside of the cardboard body using tape.
  5. Inflate the balloon, but don't tie it. Tape it to the top of the car, with the opening facing the back.

6. Inflate the balloon and then let it go. Watch your car speed forward, powered by wind!

CARDBOARD ELEVATOR PROJECT

And now something very cool. Let's build our very own elevator. It will be a little bit challenging, but the result will be great. I know you can do it! Here's what we need and how to make it:

- **Materials:**
    - A sturdy cardboard box
    - String
    - One short stick and two long sticks (30cm each) - you can use wire if you don't have sticks; just be careful and ask for an adult's help to cut it.
    - Scissors
    - Hot glue or tape and a glue stick
    - Pliers (if you're using wire)
    - A straw
    - A paperclip
- **Steps:**

1. Make the Elevator Cube: Cut five cardboard squares (7x7 cm each). Stick them together to form a cube with one open side. Use hot glue for a stronger hold, but tape works, too, if you're uncomfortable with it.
2. Create the Elevator Shaft: Cut out pieces to make the elevator box: one 30x9 cm strip, two 8.5x30 cm strips, and two 9x9 cm squares (for the floor and ceiling of the elevator).
3. Attach the Elevator: Cut two holes at the top of your elevator shaft and pass the long sticks through them, inserting the elevator. Seal the stick entrances with glue or tape.
4. Make a Simple Gear: Cut three cardboard circles - two with a 6 cm diameter and one with 5 cm. Make a hole in the center of each and stack them, placing the smallest in the middle. Glue them together. Thread the straw through the center and trim it so it only shows in the middle of the circles. This will be our control gear.
5. Install the Gear: Cut two 3x3 cm squares and two triangles of cardboard for the gear supports. Attach them at the top of the elevator shaft. Place the gear between them, ensuring it rotates freely but isn't too loose. Push the short stick through the straw and secure it on the supports with glue or tape.

6. String it Up: Make a hole in the middle of the elevator's ceiling. Thread the string through it and then through the middle of the gear.
7. Final Touch: Modify the paperclip to make a semi-circle and attach it to the top of the elevator. Tie the string to the paperclip. Now, you can raise and lower your elevator by turning the gear!

When Aysel, Shani, their dad, and I embarked on our cardboard elevator project, we were really excited. Aysel and Shani were so eager to see their elevator go up and down. But, although we followed all the steps carefully when we tried it out, the elevator went up smoothly, and then, it just wouldn't come down.

We huddled together and started troubleshooting, just like real engineers. What could be wrong? After some investigation, we found that the holes on the sides of the elevator, where the long sticks were inserted, were too tight. This meant our elevator couldn't use gravity to glide back down.

So, we worked on loosening the holes a bit, giving the sticks more room to move. And guess what? It worked like a charm! Our elevator could now move up and down smoothly.

This little hiccup taught us an important lesson: things might not be perfect on your first try, and that's completely okay; every moment is an opportunity to learn. Aysel and Shani learned a lot about problem-solving and the value of perseverance. Even if your project doesn't work perfectly at first, every step you take is a step towards learning something new. That's the real fun of engineering and experimenting!

MATH IN DAILY LIFE

Math is everywhere, and it can be really entertaining. We often picture numbers and equations when we think of math, but there is much more. Like solving real-life puzzles, figuring out how to spend your allowance wisely, or planning a fabulous family trip. It's about intelligent shopping, ensuring you get the most out of your money, seeing the beauty in the world, like the perfect patterns in a flower, or creating your own artistic masterpiece with shapes and colors. So, let's enter into these everyday adventures and see how math makes them even more exciting!

TIME MANAGEMENT

Have you ever wondered how to figure out how much time you have left to play before dinner or how long a movie will last? Understanding clocks, calendars, and schedules is a big part of our daily lives, and it's all related to math! When we look at a clock, we're actually doing math, adding and subtracting hours and minutes.

For example, let's say you start watching a movie at 6 PM that's 2 hours long. You can use addition to figure out it will end at 8 PM; if you're planning a day out and need to be back by 6 PM, but it's now 3 PM, subtraction helps you know you have 3 hours left to enjoy. Understanding elapsed time, like how long a trip takes from start to finish, also involves math. It's a different way to manage your time and make the most out of every day!

GEOMETRY IN NATURE AND ART

Math is, of course, numbers, but it is also in the beautiful shapes around us. Take a look at the flowers in the garden. Do you notice their symmetrical petals? That's geometry in action. When you draw or paint, the shapes you use, like circles, triangles, and squares, are all geometry. When you understand these shapes, you can create unique art. And just like any skill, getting good at geometry is about practice, not just being a "math person." Then, why not try to explore and create some geometric art?

TRAVEL PLANNING

Planning a trip can be a blast, especially when you throw in some math! Imagine your family is planning a road trip. How long will the journey take if your car travels 60 miles in an hour and your destination is 180 miles away? Just divide the distance by the speed ($180 \div 60$), and voilà, it's a 3-hour journey! This is how math helps in real life. The key is understanding and practicing simple math concepts.

Budgeting Allowance

Your allowance is to buy some snacks or toys, and it also helps you start budgeting! Imagine you get $10 a week. How about saving $3 for something big you want? Then you have $7 left. Maybe spend $4 on something fun now and save the rest? See, budgeting is like a puzzle, figuring out how to use your money smartly. Being good at math doesn't mean you need to be a genius; you need to practice, just like budgeting. The more you do it, the better you get!

Shopping Skills

Let's turn shopping into a fun math challenge. Imagine you have $20 to buy a new book. The book costs $18, but there's a 10% discount. How much will the book cost now? First, find 10% of $18 ($1.80), then subtract that from $18. The answer is $16.20. Now you know you'll have some change left for a snack! This is how math helps us make smart shopping decisions. As with many other things in life, it's a matter of time to gain confidence in math.

Each time you use math, whether it's in time management or shopping, you're building your mathematical confidence. Always remember that every problem you solve and every figure you calculate is a step towards becoming more skilled in math. So, keep practicing, stay curious, and watch how math can become your superpower in the real world!

GEMS Superstars: Shattering Ceilings with Inspiring Tales

Now, let's talk about amazing women! Did you know some super cool women have done amazing things in Science, Technology, Engineering, and Math (STEM)? Let me tell you about them!

Science: Marie Curie

Marie Curie was a super genius in science! She discovered not one but two elements: radium and polonium. Even though people didn't always take her seriously; she showed them all her value by becoming the first woman to win a Nobel Prize, and she didn't stop there because she won it twice in two different science fields!

Marie teaches us that if you love science and work hard, you can make amazing discoveries and contributions to science, no matter what anyone else says!

TECHNOLOGY: KATHERINE JOHNSON

Imagine being so good at math that you help send astronauts to the moon! That's what Katherine Johnson did. She worked for NASA, and her superb math skills were crucial for the Apollo 11 mission to land on the moon. It wasn't easy. She broke through barriers to reach for the stars!

Katherine's story shows that your brainpower can take you to the moon and back. So dream big, study hard, and maybe you'll help the next astronaut land on Mars!

ENGINEERING: ELLEN OCHOA

Ellen Ochoa is a trailblazing astronaut with roots proudly reaching back to Mexico. She wasn't just the first Hispanic woman to go to space; she also invented technology to help spacecraft see the Earth in new ways. Ellen soared above the Earth in a space shuttle, showing us the sky's not the limit!

Ellen's journey tells us that your heritage is a significant part of you and that no matter where you

come from, you can reach the stars and beyond. So, grab your space helmet; we've got galaxies to explore!

MATHEMATICS: ADA LOVELACE

Ada Lovelace was way ahead of her time. She wrote the world's first computer program a hundred years before computers were even invented. She saw a world where computers could do more than just math, and she was right!

Ada's life is a reminder that math can be like a secret code that can unlock the future. Who knows what amazing things you'll discover with it?

These stories are just a sneak peek into the world of women who rocked STEM. They show us that science, tech, engineering, and math are for everyone, especially for girls like you who are curious, creative, and ready to explore the unknown! Let these incredible women inspire us and dream big!

WRAP-UP

Wow, what a fantastic adventure we've had in Chapter 3! We've navigated into the fascinating world of STEM, exploring everything from cool science experiments in our kitchens to programming our first computer games. We built our little engineering marvels and discovered how math is an incredible tool in our daily lives. And most importantly, we've been inspired by the stunning women who've broken barriers in STEM, showing us that these fields are definitely for girls.

Every experiment, every line of code, and every math problem solved is a step towards a future where you, yes YOU, can be a scientist, a tech whiz, an engineer, or a math expert. So keep exploring, keep learning, and remember, the world of STEM is waiting for you to make your mark.

CHAPTER FOUR

AMAZING SPORTS!

Sports are a great way to stay fit, make friends, and learn new skills. Here, we're going to explore a variety of sports, including some you might think aren't for you. But guess what? They're for everyone!

SPORTS!

ATHLETICS: INDIVIDUAL CHALLENGE AND VERSATILITY

Athletics is the ultimate test of personal challenge. Whether you're sprinting, jumping, or throwing, it's about setting and breaking personal records. Girls who participate in athletics experience a wide range of activities, each requiring different skills. It's a sport where you can constantly challenge yourself, improve your fitness, and enjoy the thrill of competition.

CRICKET: STRATEGIC PLAY AND TEAM SPIRIT

Cricket is a game of patience and strategy, and girls who play cricket learn the art of thinking ahead, working as a team, and enjoying the slow, strategic nature of the game. It's a sport of precision, whether you're batting, bowling, or fielding. And there's a real sense of achievement in understanding and mastering the various aspects of this classic sport.

MARTIAL ARTS: DISCIPLINE AND CONFIDENCE

Martial arts are very much related to self-defense, but there is more. They teach discipline, respect, and inner strength. For girls, martial arts can be an empowering journey to discover their strength and resilience. You will learn to stand tall, respect others, and confidently face challenges. Plus, it's a fantastic way to stay fit and focused, a true blend of mind, body, and spirit.

BASKETBALL: HIGH ENERGY AND COORDINATION

Dribble, shoot, score! Basketball is a dynamic sport that combines fitness with fun, where girls can develop quick reflexes, coordination, and a keen sense of strategy. It's a high-energy game where every basket scored is a triumph of teamwork and personal skill. Plus, it's a fantastic way to boost your senses and coordination, showing that you can jump as high and play as hard as your maximum effort.

SKATEBOARDING: FREEDOM ON WHEELS

Skateboarding is a sport but also a form of expression. For girls who love adventure and creativity, skateboarding offers a unique way to express their freedom, balance, and the thrill of mastering a new trick. Every ollie and grind of your nail is a step towards self-discovery and confidence. And the best part? You get to show the world that skateboarding has style and spirit!

SOCCER: THE TEAM BUILDER

Why play soccer? Because it is an excellent and fun game! You will enjoy being part of a team, chasing a shared goal (literally!), and feeling the thrill of teamwork. Girls in soccer learn to trust, cooperate, and celebrate together. Every pass, goal, or save strengthens your body and your bond with your teammates. Here, you can run, strategize, laugh, and score, all while building lifelong friendships.

Swimming: Personal Goals and Water Fun

Swimming is like a splash of joy! It's perfect for girls who love to set personal goals and achieve them stroke by stroke. No matter if you are a beginner enjoying the feeling of water for the first time or you are a pro, swimming is about personal growth and fun. It's a full-body workout that improves your strength and stamina, all while having a great time in the pool.

Discover the Magic of Yoga

Ready to embark on a magical yoga journey? Yoga is more than just striking poses; it's a thrilling adventure where you'll discover your inner strength and flexibility. All in your body but especially in your mind and emotions, too! Imagine being a warrior one minute and a peaceful tree the next. Yoga is all about finding balance and joy in every moment.

Become Strong, Supple, and Steady

Close your eyes and try to feel strong, flexible, and super balanced. That's what yoga does! It's like having a superpower where you gently build your muscles, make yourself as bendy as a gymnast, and learn to balance like a pro. Each pose is a new challenge, a new chance to feel amazing in your own skin.

Clear Your Mind and Sharpen Your Focus

Have you ever wished you could clear away all the buzzing thoughts and have a clear focus? Here, you have yoga! With cool breathing exercises and calming meditations, you'll learn to sweep away the fuzziness and sharpen your mind. It's like having a magic wand to help you concentrate on homework, remember cool facts, and organize your thoughts.

Ride the Emotional Rollercoaster Like a Champ

Life's full of twists and turns, but guess what? Yoga turns you into an emotional ninja. Feeling stressed or worried? Yoga's relaxation tricks have your back, helping you chill out and find your smile. Plus, it's a fantastic way to learn about positive thinking and loving yourself just as you are.

Yoga's not just about connecting with yourself; it helps you share the fun and peace with others. Whether practicing poses with friends or teaching your family a cool breathing trick, with yoga, you have a way to bring people together, like a secret recipe for happiness and calm that you can share with everyone!

START YOUR OWN YOGA ADVENTURE

Get ready to become a yoga explorer. Here, I share some fun and easy poses you can try right in your room. In yoga, you are not competing to be the best; you will look to enjoy yourself and feel fantastic. These are some cool beginner poses that will kick-start your yoga adventure with a bang!

FUN YOGA POSES FOR BEGINNERS

Yoga is a terrific way to stretch your body, relax your mind, and have fun! You can try the next poses in your room. Remember that the best part about yoga is doing what feels good for you; therefore, don't worry about being perfect.

Tree Pose (Vrikshasana)

Stand on your right leg, then place your left foot on your right ankle, calf, or thigh (just not on your knee). Raise your arms like branches reaching for the sky. This pose helps with balance and focus, making you feel strong and rooted like a tree!

Warrior Pose (Virabhadrasana)

Step one foot back and bend your front knee, keeping your back leg straight. Reach your arms out to the sides like a warrior ready for action. This pose builds strength in your legs and arms and makes you feel super powerful.

Lotto Flower Pose (Baddha Konasana)

Sit down, bring the soles of your feet together, cross your legs, and let your knees drop out to the sides. This gentle pose is excellent for opening your hips and makes you feel like a beautiful butterfly spreading its wings.

Downward-Facing Dog (Adho Mukha Svanasana)

From your hands and knees, lift your hips high to form an upside-down 'V' with your body. This pose stretches your legs and back and gives you a feeling of energy as it improves blood flow to your head.

Each of these poses has something unique to offer your body and mind. No matter if you are building strength, improving balance, or just having a moment to relax, with yoga, you have a fantastic way to take care of yourself. Plus, it's amusing! So, why not give these poses a chance and see how you feel?

BRING YOGA INTO YOUR EVERYDAY LIFE

The best part? You can sprinkle a little bit of yoga magic into your everyday life! Simple things like a morning stretch, a deep breath before a test, or even standing tall like a tree while waiting in line are all mini-yoga moments.

GIRLS MAKING STRIDES IN SPORTS

Ever felt like some sports are not for you? Well, guess what? That's not true at all! Sports are for everyone! Let me share some amazing stories of athletes who didn't let anything stand in their way!

Overcoming Stereotypes: The Story of Serena Williams

Serena Williams, a name synonymous with strength and skill in tennis, had to contend with more than just tough opponents on the court. Early in her career, Serena faced criticism about her body, her style of play, and even her attire, challenging norms in a sport steeped in tradition. Despite these obstacles, Serena used her decisive game, an unrelenting determination, and her unique flair to dominate tennis and change how female athletes are perceived. Her journey showed us that facing and overcoming stereotypes can lead to groundbreaking success. In conclusion, never let stereotypes stop you from playing the sport you love!

Dealing with Doubt: Simone Biles' Journey

Simone Biles, an Olympic gymnastics icon, had no easy path to gold medals and global acclaim. She battled against early doubts about her small stature and overcame personal challenges, including time in foster care. But she turned her height into her superpower, flipping and flying through the air like a superhero. Simone's journey was one of turning every doubt into a stepping stone for success, demonstrating how perceived weaknesses can be transformed into unmatched strengths.

Embracing Different Abilities: Jessica Long's Inspiring Swim

Jessica Long's journey to becoming a Paralympic swimming legend involved more than just training and discipline. Born without lower legs, Jessica underwent numerous surgeries throughout her childhood. She faced the challenge of adapting to prosthetics, not just in daily life but also in competitive swimming. She became one of the most decorated Paralympic athletes ever. Her remarkable story isn't just related to winning medals but to the relentless pursuit of excellence in the face of extraordinary personal challenges.

Shattering Barriers: Laurie Hernandez's Gymnastic Triumphs

Laurie Hernandez, a gymnast of Puerto Rican descent, is a shining example of practice and determination. At a young age, Laurie faced the challenge of fitting into a sport where few athletes looked like her. But she didn't let that stop her. With her dazzling smile and incredible talent, she became a part of the "Final Five" U.S. women's gymnastics team, winning gold and silver medals at the 2016 Olympics. Laurie's story teaches us about embracing our heritage and reaching for the stars, no matter where we come from.

SOCCER: MARTA VIEIRA DA SILVA'S REMARKABLE JOURNEY

Marta Vieira da Silva, known simply as Marta, is a Brazilian soccer legend. Growing up in a humble background, Marta played street soccer with the boys, often being the only girl on the field. She didn't let gender norms hold her back; her incredible skills made her one of the greatest female soccer players ever, earning the title of FIFA World Player of the Year six times. Marta's story is a testament to determination and breaking through barriers.

WRAP-UP

From exploring a variety of sports in "Amazing Sports!" and shattering stereotypes to delving into the transformative world of yoga in "Discover the Magic of Yoga," we've uncovered the boundless potential of our bodies and minds. In this chapter, we also have met inspirational athletes who have shown us that with determination, passion, and courage, girls can excel in any sport and break down any barrier.

The most important part of this chapter was not about learning new sports or yoga poses but about discovering our inner strength, fostering our confidence, and realizing that the field, court, or yoga mat is where we can all shine. Each sport, each pose, and each story we have encountered is a reminder that girls have the power to defy expectations and make a mark in the world of sports and beyond. So, let's carry this spirit of adventure, wellness, and resilience with us as we continue to explore, grow, and challenge ourselves in every aspect of our lives. Then, keep playing, stretching, and breaking barriers because, girls, the world is ours to conquer!

CHAPTER FIVE

CREATIVE AND ARTISTIC EXPRESSION

Welcome to Chapter 5, "Creative and Artistic Expression"! In this chapter, we will explore a world where colors, shapes, sounds, and movements come alive. Maybe you love strumming a guitar, painting a sunset, or acting in a play. In this chapter, you will read about the importance of expressing yourself and embracing your inner artist. So, grab your gear, and let's get ready to create, perform, and shine!

UNLEASHING YOUR INNER ARTIST!

Art is a way to express what is inside you through different colors, shapes, and even words. We will start by exploring the magic of light and color because these two elements bring life to all art forms, like a colorful painting, a stunning photograph, or even the design of your favorite video game.

THE POWER OF LIGHT AND COLOR IN ART

- **Light:** It is like the magic wand of art. Using light, you can create mood, depth, and emotion. In photography, for instance, light can transform a simple object into a masterpiece. In painting, it can make your artwork feel happy, sad, or mysterious.
- **Color:** Colors speak without words. Red can show passion or danger, blue can be calming or sad, and yellow can make us feel happy and energetic. Mixing colors is like mixing emotions; using them wisely, you can create new feelings and stories.

- **Materials:** White paper, colored cellophane sheets (or any transparent colored material), a flashlight, and objects like toys or leaves.
- **Steps:**

  1. Place an object on the paper.
  2. Shine the flashlight through a colored cellophane sheet onto the object to cast a colored shadow.
  3. Trace the shadow with a pencil or marker.
  4. Repeat with different colors and objects, creating a layered, colorful shadow art piece.

ART PROJECT: MY DREAM WORLD COLLAGE

Imagine creating your dream world where everything you love and dream about comes to life! That's what we will do with this fun art project: a Dream World Collage. Think about it as a treasure map to your heart, filled with all your favorite things and wildest dreams!

- **Treasure Hunt for Materials:** First, we need some awesome stuff for our collage. Look for old magazines, colorful papers, stickers, or even bits of fabric. Find pictures or words that make you smile or think of your dreams. Don't forget scissors, glue, and a big piece of cardboard for your masterpiece.

- **What's Your Dream?** Think about what you love and dream about. Is it space travel, deep-sea adventures, or a world where animals can talk? Your collage is going to show all of this!
- **Cutting and Pasting Fun:** Start cutting out all the cool stuff you found. Arrange them on your cardboard like a puzzle, but don't glue them yet. Move them around and make it look just like the dream world in your head.
- **Background Magic:** If you want, you can color or draw on the cardboard first. Maybe you want a rainbow background or a starry night? Let your imagination run wild!
- **Stick it All Down:** Start sticking everything down when you're super happy with how it looks. Make sure everything is flat and neat.
- **Add Your Magic Touch:** Now for the best part! Add your drawings or special little things like a movie ticket or a note from your best friend. This makes it extra special and all about you.
- **Show it Off:** Find the perfect spot in your room to hang your dream world. It's a piece of art that's all about you and your amazing dreams!
- **Think About Your Creation:** After you're done, consider what you made. Why did you pick each piece? What story does it tell? Your collage is like a window into your dreams, and it's as unique and special as you are.

Creating your Dream World Collage is an art and also a way to explore who you are and what you dream about. It's a journey to a world where anything is possible, and you're the artist who brings it to life!!

Writing as Art

Writing is not just for school essays or homework; it is an art form where words paint pictures and emotions and create amazing stories, share dreams, and create new worlds!

Project: My Storybook Adventure

1. **Choose Your Theme:** Begin by selecting a theme that lights up your imagination. It could be friendship, adventure, courage, or anything else that speaks to you. Ask yourself, what message do I want to share? Is it about the power of dreams, the magic of teamwork, or the thrill of discovery? Find inspiration in your hobbies, dreams, or recent learnings.
2. **Create Your Characters:** Who are the stars of your story? Imagine the heroes of your story. They can be people, animals, magical creatures, or anything you dream up! Give them names, personalities, and unique traits. Think about what they love, fear, and dream of. Create a 'character sheet' for each one, detailing their looks, hobbies, likes, dislikes, family, and special qualities.
3. **Set the Scene:** Where does your story happen? Describe where your story unfolds. It could be anywhere: a bustling city, a serene village, a mystical forest, or an unknown planet. Use all five senses to paint this world. What can be seen, heard, smelled, touched, and tasted? Also, consider the time setting – is it in the present, past, or a fantastical future? Describe a typical day in this world for vivid imagery.
4. **Plot Your Story:** What happens in your story? Outline a story with a beginning, middle, and end. Start with an introduction (setting and characters), then build up to a problem or challenge (rising action). Reach a thrilling moment (climax), follow it with efforts towards solving the problem (falling action), and conclude with a resolution. Think of a unique challenge for your characters and how they will resolve it.
5. **Create an original end:** Surprise your readers with an unconventional ending. Maybe the perceived enemy becomes a friend, or the journey teaches more than the goal itself. Be creative and challenge common story conclusions.
6. **Add Dialogue and Details:** Bring your story to life with dialogue and rich descriptions. Show emotions and actions through words and interactions. Instead of telling the reader what to feel, show them through your characters' experiences, conversations, and thoughts. Make your story vibrant and engaging.

7. **Illustrate Your Story:** Draw pictures for your storybook. These can be simple sketches or elaborate drawings, whatever you like. They will add a visual element to your story, making it even more special.
8. **Assemble Your Storybook:** Put your story and illustrations together. You can staple pages, tie them with ribbon, or even create a digital version.
9. **Share Your Story:** Read your storybook to family, friends, or even your class. Sharing your creation can be a proud and joyous moment.
10. **Commit to Writing Regularly:** Try to write for at least 20 minutes each day. Setting aside a little time every day to work on your story will help you finish it. Remember, the more you write, the better your story will become!

The beauty of writing is that it lets you create entire worlds with just words. Your storybook is like a canvas for your creativity, a place where anything you imagine can come to life. So grab your pen, and let's start creating!

MUSIC AND PERFORMANCE ARTS

Are you ready to explore the fantastic world of Music and Performance Arts? Here, you can express yourself, tell your story, and even step into someone else's shoes! Come and see the magic of music, drama, dance and discover how they can transform us and the world.

MUSIC: MELODIES OF EXPRESSION

- Instruments & Singing: Whether strumming a guitar, tickling the ivories on a piano, or lifting your voice, learning an instrument or singing can be a thrilling momentum! Each note you play or sing is like a painting with sound.
- Music Composition: How about writing your song? You can be an author but with melodies and rhythms! You can express your feelings, tell a story, or just create something that sounds cool. There's no right or wrong in music; it matters what feels right to you.

DRAMA: THE STAGE IS YOURS

- Acting: Stepping into a character's shoes helps you see the world differently. It could be a play or maybe an improvisation game with your friends; acting helps you explore emotions, situations, and characters in a safe and creative environment.
- Scriptwriting: Fancy creating your own play? Scriptwriting lets you weave stories, craft dialogues, and bring characters to life. It's a powerful way to share your ideas and imagination with others.

DANCE: RHYTHM IN MOTION

- Different Dance Forms: From ballet to hip-hop, from folk dances to contemporary, each style tells a story through movement. Dancing is steps, rhythm, and music inside you and gives you a way to express yourself through your body.
- Choreography: Like a painter with a blank canvas, you can create your own dance! In choreography, you combine movements to make a dance that can tell a story and express an emotion. It's exciting and deeply personal; your dance reflects your unique self.

EMBRACE YOUR ARTISTIC SELF!

Remember, girls, these artistic skills are a way to connect with yourself and others. They help you build self-esteem, express your feelings, and see the world through a creative lens. You might be belting out a tune, acting in a play, or dancing every time you're learning, growing, and, most importantly, having a blast!

So, what are you waiting for? Grab that microphone, step onto the stage, or slip on your dancing shoes. Let's make the world our stage and show everyone the power of our artistic voices!

EXPLORING DIGITAL ARTS: THE NEW FRONTIER OF CREATIVITY

Alright, after exploring traditional arts and the performing arts, let's step into the fascinating world of Digital Arts, a place where your creativity meets the endless possibilities of technology. We will discover how to use digital tools like tablets and computers to bring your artistic ideas to life. Think of it as having an endless supply of colors, shapes, and possibilities right at your fingertips. We'll explore the basics of digital painting, animation, and even game design, pushing the boundaries of your imagination and seeing your art in a whole new light. Are you ready to explore this new frontier of creativity?

YOUR FIRST DIGITAL MASTERPIECE

Come and create your very first digital artwork. We will use cool, kid-friendly apps that make digital art fun and easy. Let's dive in and unleash your inner digital Picasso!

1. Choose Your App: We'll start with a user-friendly app like 'Tux Paint' or 'SketchBook'; these are perfect for beginners and have lots of fun. Make sure to get a grown-up to help you download and install it.

2. Familiarize Yourself with the Tools: Once you've opened the app, take a little time to play around. Check out the different brushes, colors, and shapes. It's like your digital art toolbox!

3. Start with a Simple Project: Let's begin with something fun, like drawing a cartoon version of your pet or creating a colorful landscape. Use basic shapes to build your drawing. Remember, there's no 'right' way to do art; just have fun with it!

4. Add Colors and Details: Now, bring your drawing to life with colors! Experiment with different shades and see how they change the mood of your artwork. Add details like shadows or highlights to make it pop.

5. Save Your Masterpiece: Once you're happy with your artwork, save it! You can give it a cool name, too.

6. Sharing Your Art Safely Online: If you want to share your art with friends or family, let's discuss internet safety. Always ask a parent or guardian before you post anything online. And remember, it's best to share your art in safe, kid-friendly spaces or with people you know.

7. Feedback and Fun: Share your art and see what others think! Getting feedback is a great way to learn and improve. And don't forget to check out other kids' art, too, for inspiration.

There you go! You've just created your first piece of digital art. How amazing is that? Remember, each piece you make is a step forward in your artistic journey.

WRAP-UP

As we close this chapter on Creative and Artistic Expression, let's take a moment to reflect on the incredible journey of discovery and self-expression we've embarked on. From the swirls of paint on a canvas to the rhythm of a dance, from the melody of a song to the strokes of a digital pen, each activity has been a step towards uncovering the diverse art world surrounding us. Every form of art you explore is a language in itself, a unique way to communicate your feelings, thoughts, and dreams for your present and your future.

Think back to the first time you picked up a brush when you first danced to your favorite tune, or even when you crafted your first story or poem. Each of these moments was an opportunity to create something beautiful and find a piece of yourself in everyone. Art, in all its forms, allows us to explore and understand our emotions, to connect with others, and to see the world through a kaleidoscope of perspectives.

And don't forget the lessons we learned in digital arts. As we step further into the digital age, your ability to blend traditional art forms with new technologies will open doors to endless possibilities. The digital world is vast, and navigating it creatively and safely is essential for the modern artist. Your journey into digital arts is just beginning, and the potential for innovation and creation is limitless.

Creativity has no boundaries as you continue on your artistic journey of mixing, matching, and blending in different art forms. Maybe you'll find your passion in a traditional art form like painting or something more contemporary like digital animation. Or perhaps you'll discover a love for a combination of both. The key is to keep experimenting, learning, and growing as an artist.

As we turn the last page of this chapter, take with you the curiosity, excitement, and joy that art brings. Sometimes, in a quiet corner with a sketchpad, maybe on a lively stage, or even behind a computer screen, your artistic journey is uniquely yours. Embrace, cherish, and let it be a source of joy and expression throughout your life.

CHAPTER SIX

GROWING AS LEADERS: FINDING YOUR VOICE

It is time for Chapter 6., where we will embark on an empowering journey to discover the leader within each of us. We'll learn how to develop essential leadership qualities like consciousness, courage, and compassion.

Then, we'll enter into ethical decision-making and learn the art of working collaboratively with others. Public speaking will become our super skill as we practice how to express our thoughts and opinions confidently. And there is more! We'll get hands-on with exciting activities like role-playing, group projects, and inspiring discussions about female leaders who have made a mark in various fields.

Well, get ready to raise your voice, make a difference, and lead the way because every girl has the potential to be a great leader!

STEPPING INTO LEADERSHIP!

Leadership is not only for grown-ups; no matter the age, you can start learning right now. Like a newborn superhero, it is a process of discovering your powers, where you will end up finding the leader within you.

In this journey, we will understand ourselves, grow from past and present experiences, and care for those around us. We will explore some incredible qualities that will have the power to transform us into a fantastic leader, and guess what? I'm sure you might already have some of these powers! So, let's unlock your leadership potential together.

SELF-AWARENESS

- Being a leader starts with knowing yourself. This is like having a friendship with your inner self, which means understanding your feelings and figuring out what makes you feel happy, sad, or frustrated. Just as you get to know a friend, getting to know yourself helps you make better decisions and be a more conscious leader.
- Tip to practice: Keep a diary where you write about your day. This helps you understand your feelings better and see how you react to different situations.

SELF-IMPROVEMENT

- Imagine you're an Olympic Athlete, always practicing and growing stronger! Self-improvement is about always trying to be your best self, which could mean learning new things, being more careful, and even admitting when you make a mistake. Every step you take to improve helps you become a fantastic leader.
- Tip to practice: Set small goals for things you want to improve, like learning a new skill or being kinder to a sibling. Celebrate when you achieve these goals!

KEEPING CALM IN STRESSFUL MOMENTS

- Sometimes, things get tough, but a cool-headed leader can make all the difference. Imagine a steady captain of a ship in a storm. When you're calm, you can think clearly and help others feel safe, too.
- Tip to practice: Practice deep breathing or count to ten when you feel stressed. This can help calm your mind.

EMPATHY

- Understanding how others feel is super important, and you can do it by imagining that you are using their shoes to see the world from their perspective. When you show empathy, your friends and teammates will feel heard and valued, which is a big part of being a good leader. However, it is critical to remember that you can't help anyone if you do not help yourself first. You need to be kind to yourself to be ready to help others.
- Tip to practice: Try to put yourself in others' shoes. When a friend is sad, think about how you would feel in their situation and what would make you feel better.

INTENTION TO IMPACT

- Every action we take affects others, the same way as dropping a pebble in the water creates the ripples that then spread out. Always think about how your actions might impact you and those around you. What kind of impact do you want? Maybe helping a friend or starting a recycling project at school is a good start for a positive one.
- Tip to practice: Create a 'Decision Tree' where you map out the possible outcomes of your choices. This helps you see the impact of your decisions.

TEAMWORK TRIUMPHS: ETHICS AND COLLABORATION

Time to learn about making choices that are good for everyone and working together like a dream team. What ethical decision-making and collaboration mean is that we need to choose what's right and team up for the best results. When thinking and working as a united group, we can make extraordinary choices and work together brilliantly!

UNDERSTANDING ETHICAL DECISION-MAKING

Ethical decision-making is a way of looking at a world that steps up for fairness and kindness. It means thinking about what is right and wrong and making choices that are good for everyone and not just for us.

THE CHOICE GAME

Create a simple board game with squares colored Green, Red, Yellow, and Blue, leading from "Start" to "Finish." Prepare four sets of 4 cards each: Green for clearly good choices, Red for not-so-good choices, Yellow for tricky decisions, and Blue for

Bonus cards. Some choices are clearly good (like helping a friend), some are clearly not so good (like keeping a found object without trying to find its owner), and some are tricky (like choosing between two good options). Players will move using small objects or tokens as game pieces. They will take turns rolling a die to move forward. When landing on a square, draw a card from the corresponding-colored pile. The player must discuss what they would do in each scenario, focusing on the impact of their decision. After discussing their choice, players can move extra spaces for good decisions or stay put for not-so-good choices.

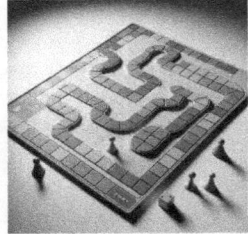

The game encourages discussing why certain choices are better, promoting ethical thinking and empathy. The first player to reach the last square is the winner, but the real victory is in the thoughtful discussions and learning. Ensure that an adult is present to guide discussions, especially for tricky or sensitive scenarios.

Here you have options for your choice-colored cards:

Green Cards (Good Choices):

1. Helping a New Student: You notice a new student looking lost. Do you guide them to their next class?
2. Found Money: You find $5 on the school grounds. Do you turn it into the lost and found?
3. Recycling Efforts: You see someone throwing a plastic bottle in the trash. Do you pick it up and put it in the recycling bin?
4. Inclusion in Play: A classmate is often left out during recess. Do you invite them to join your game?

Red Cards (Not So Good Choices):

1. Homework Dilemma: You forgot to do your homework. Do you copy a friend's work without asking?
2. Littering: You have a wrapper, but no trash can nearby. Do you drop the wrapper on the ground?
3. Ignoring a Problem: You witness bullying but feel scared. Do you pretend not to see and walk away?
4. Breaking the rules: Your friends dare you to climb a fence into a restricted area. Do you go along with the dare?

Yellow Cards (Tricky Choices):

1. Birthday Party vs. Family Event: You're invited to a best friend's birthday party, but it's on the same day as a family reunion. Which do you choose?
2. Group Project Leader: Two friends want to lead the next group project. Whom do you support?
3. Extra Credit Work: You can do extra credit for a class, but it means you might miss your sibling's sports game. What do you decide?
4. Found Item: You see a pretty necklace without identification at the park. Do you keep it, or try to find the owner?

Blue Bonus Cards (Mix of Choices):

1. Charity Money: You've saved $10. Do you spend it on a new toy or donate to a charity?
2. Helping an Injured Animal: You find a hurt bird. Do you try to help it, even if you might be late for school?
3. Sharing a Secret: A friend tells you a secret, but it's something that worries you. Do you keep it to yourself or tell a trusted adult?
4. Library Book: You borrowed a book from a friend and accidentally spilled juice. Do you apologize and offer to replace it, or hope they don't notice?

LEARNING ABOUT COLLABORATION

When we work together like a unified team, we call it collaboration. We care to listen to each other, share ideas, and build something unique in unison with a clear goal and objectives.

Dream Team Project: Form small groups and choose a project to work on together, like a mini science experiment, a new game, an art piece, or even a challenging new video game. Discuss, plan, and create together, focusing on how each member contributes to the team.

CONCLUSION

Making good choices and working with others are skills we will use our entire lives. With them, we can make a big difference in our world by thinking about what's fair and joining forces with others who think alike. Every decision we make is a step towards being a better leader.

Speak Up: Making Your Voice Heard!

Hey there, future world changers! Have you ever dreamed of standing in front of an audience, sharing your brilliant ideas, and having everyone listen intently? That's the power of public speaking! We are not talking about speaking loudly but expressing our thoughts in a clear and exciting way. It might be a class presentation, speaking at a school assembly, or sharing a story with friends or family. In all those situations, your voice matters, and I'm happy to share with you some of my tips and activities that would help you become a captivating speaker.

The Power of Your Voice

Let me start with a very basic but important topic. What is public speaking in reality? Well, it is when you stand up and share your thoughts, stories, or ideas with others, and it can be in front of a small group or a big crowd. You might be wondering, "What am I going to say that might be important?" or "Just adults can do that." But hey, guess what? You don't have to be a grown-up to have amazing things to say. Your ideas, dreams, and stories are essential right now at your age.

Public speaking is super cool because it lets you share a part of yourself with others. You open your thoughts as if you were opening a treasure and let others see the gems inside. And the best part? When you share your ideas, you might inspire someone else. Maybe you'll talk about saving the environment, your favorite book, or how to solve a tricky math problem. Whatever it is, it's your unique perspective, and that's pretty awesome.

Then, don't wait until you're older to start speaking up. Your voice is powerful today. Maybe in class, at a club meeting, or at the dinner with your family, you have the magic of words at your fingertips. When you speak, you're inspiring, teaching, and connecting with others; let's turn your beautiful thoughts into words that everyone can hear.

Crafting Your Message

First things first. Have you ever had a super cool idea but weren't sure how to share it with others? That's where crafting your message comes in! You just need to know how to organize your thoughts and transform them into insightful words able to shine and engage your listeners.

How to Build Your Message Like a Pro!

- **Pick Your Passion:** Start with something you love, maybe your favorite book, your favorite artist, a remarkable science fact, or your dream vacation spot with your family. There you have it; that is your golden topic!
- **Brainstorm Bonanza:** Now, grab a piece of paper and jot down all the things you can think about your golden topic. Write everything that comes to your mind. No idea is too wild!
- **Map It Out: Now,** let's sort those ideas. Which ones make your heart race with excitement? Put those at the top! This is your message's map.
- **The Beginning, Middle, and End:** Every great story has a start (introduce your topic), a middle (share all those fantastic details), and an end (wrap it up with a neat bow). Like building a LEGO castle, each part has its place.

ACTIVITY: STORY BUILDING TIME!

Let's put your new skills to the test with a super fun activity. Create a short story or presentation about something you adore. Here's how:

- **Choose a Topic:** What makes your heart sing? Puppies? Outer space? The world's tallest cake? Pick that!
- **Create Your Storyboard:** Divide a paper into three parts: Beginning, Middle, and End. Sketch or write your ideas in each part.
- **Add Color and Flair:** Decorate your storyboard. Stickers, drawings, and glitter make it uniquely yours.
- **Present Your Masterpiece:** Share your story with someone. It could be your family, friends, or even your stuffed animals. Stand tall, speak clearly, and let your excitement shine through!

Remember, your voice and ideas are like stars in the sky, unique and brilliant. So, let's get creative and make your message sparkle!

VOICE AND BODY LANGUAGE: EXPRESS YOURSELF!

The volume of your voice and how you move are key in public speaking. They help express your feelings and thoughts in a way that everyone understands.

- Your Voice is Powerful: A clear and strong voice makes people listen and understand your message better. Practicing different tones helps you emphasize your points.
- Body Talks Too: Your posture, gestures, and facial expressions say a lot! Standing tall shows confidence, and using your hands can help explain your ideas.
- Experiment with Your Voice: Write a few sentences on any topic you like. Read your script in different tones. Try a happy, excited tone, then a serious, thoughtful one. Notice how the tone changes the message.
- Add Body Language: Now, add gestures and expressions. If you're talking about something exciting, use big, lively gestures. If it's a serious topic, try slower, more deliberate movements.
- The Difference: Discuss with a friend or family member how the changes in your voice and body language made your message stronger or different.

ACTIVITY: MIRROR TALK CHALLENGE!

This is a fun challenge Aysel and Shani really like. Here's what you'll do:

- Choose a Topic: Write a topic you want in the paper.
- Set a Timer: Ready, set, go! You've got 2 minutes to talk about your topic.
- Watch and Learn: As you speak, watch yourself in the mirror. Notice your expressions and how you become more confident as you talk.

The more you practice, the better you'll get. And soon, you'll be speaking like a pro, not just in front of the mirror, but everywhere!

BUILDING CONFIDENCE: BECOMING YOUR OWN CHEERLEADER!

Are you feeling a little nervous about speaking out loud? Don't worry, that's totally normal! But guess what? You can become your cheerleader and boost your confidence with some tricks:

o Positive Self-Talk: Before you start speaking, give yourself a pep talk. Say things like, "I am strong, I am smart, and I can do this!" You are your best friend; talk to yourself as someone who always believes in you.
o Mirror: Stand in front of a mirror and practice your speaking as if you were having a conversation with yourself! You'll see how you look and how you move when you're sharing your thoughts.

OVERCOMING STAGE FRIGHT: TAMING THE BUTTERFLIES!

When you are about to start, you might feel frozen. That's called stage fright. It happens to almost everyone, even adults like me! But you can definitely overcome it with some tips:

o Know Your Stuff: Being prepared is vital. When you know what you want to say, you'll feel more confident.
o Deep Breathing: As we have seen before, breathing helps us to calm so before you start speaking, take a few deep breaths. It's like a mini relaxation session that calms those butterflies in your tummy.
o Start Small: Start practicing your speaking in front of a mirror, then with a pet or a stuffed animal, your sister, and your family, and slowly work your way up to other people.

ACTIVITY: FEAR BUSTER CHALLENGE!

Time to face those fears head-on with a super fun challenge:

o Prepare a Mini Speech: Think of something fun and exciting to talk about. Maybe a cool science fact, a funny story, or what you want to be when you grow up.
o Gather Your Audience: This can be your family, friends, or even your teddy bears lined up as an audience.
o Share and Reflect: Give your speech and then talk about how it felt. Were you nervous at first but then felt better as you spoke? That's progress!

Every time you speak in front of others, you're getting stronger and braver. Soon, you'll be chatting away without even a flutter of nervousness!

ACTIVITY: SURPRISE SPEAKING!

This activity is all about spontaneous speaking:

1. Prepare a List of Fun Topics: These could be anything from 'The Best Day Ever' to 'If I Were a Super Chef.'
2. Draw a Topic: Put the topics in a hat and draw one randomly.
3. Speak on the Spot: Give yourself a minute to think, then talk about the topic for two minutes.
4. Listen: Encourage everyone to offer one positive point and one suggestion for improvement.
5. Reflect and Grow: Think about the feedback you received. What can you use from it to make your next speech even better? Then, draw another topic and try again!

- o Practicing like this will make speaking in front of others feel like a breeze. So, let's start talking and turn every opportunity into a stage!
- o Feedback is a solid foundational stone to becoming a fabulous speaker; accept it with open arms and a big smile!

LEADERSHIP ACTIVITIES: YOUR TURN TO SHINE!

Did you know that all the incredible skills you've been learning are like secret ingredients for making a significant, positive splash in the world? That's right! It could be at your school, around your neighborhood, or with your circle of friends; you have the power to make things better and brighter. There is no need for a magic wand to do it; just use your newfound leadership skills.

Come with me on a trip down memory lane. Do you remember when we talked about speaking your mind confidently, making intelligent choices that are good for everyone, and working together like a dream team? These weren't just fun activities but the building blocks of being a great leader! Every time you've practiced these skills, you've been preparing to step into your leadership spotlight. There are many styles of leadership around there, but what kind of leader are you?

Every leader is unique, and like a puzzle piece, the leader finds her way to fit perfectly in the grand picture of change and innovation. Your strengths, interests, and even the things you're passionate about make you a one-of-a-kind leader. What kind are you, a creative problem-solver, a fantastic listener, or someone who brings people together like a friendship magnet?

Let's do some detective work to discover what makes you shine as a leader. Ask yourself: What are the things I love doing? Am I the first to dive into a new project or the one who makes sure everyone's voice is heard? The answers to these questions are clues to your very own leadership style.

ACTIVITY: DISCOVERING YOUR LEADERSHIP STRENGTHS!

Craft Your Quiz: Grab some paper and colorful pens. Write the following questions about what you love to do and how you react in different situations. Answer these questions honestly and creatively.

- Teamwork Test: Imagine your class is planning a big project. Do you jump in to organize the group, come up with creative ideas, or support your friends in their tasks?
- Decision Detective: You and your friends can't decide what game to play. How do you help solve the dilemma? Do you suggest a vote, develop a new game that includes everyone's ideas, or let your friends choose first?
- Adventure Attitude: When it's time to choose an activity for your family outing, what's your style? Do you list exciting options, think of something everyone will enjoy, or suggest something new and adventurous?
- Kindness Quest: What would you do if you saw a new student in your school looking lost? Would you offer to show them around, introduce them to your friends, or give them a friendly smile and a 'hello'?
- Challenge Champion: When you face a really tricky puzzle or a challenging math problem, what's your go-to strategy? Do you tackle it head-on, ask friends for ideas, or break it down into smaller, easier steps?

Analyze Your Answers: Look at your responses. Do they show you're an excellent listener, a creative thinker, or a natural organizer? Each of these qualities is a superpower in the world of leadership. Below is a short guide to help you understand your answers. Very important to know is that there's no right or wrong here, only the fantastic truth about you!

- **Teamwork Test:**

    o If you choose to organize the group, you might be a **Natural Organizer**. You're great at seeing the big picture and keeping things running smoothly.

    o If you picked coming up with creative ideas, you're likely a **Creative Thinker**. Your imagination helps you find fun solutions and new ways to do things.

    o If supporting your friends was your answer, you're an **Excellent Listener**. You understand and care about others' feelings, making you a supportive leader.

- **Decision Detective:**

    o Suggesting a vote shows you're a **Democratic Leader**. You believe everyone's opinion is important and work towards fair solutions.

    o Coming up with a new game demonstrates **Innovative Leadership**. You think outside the box and bring new ideas to the table.

    o Letting friends choose first? You're an **Altruistic Leader**. You put others' needs and happiness first.

- **Adventure Attitude:**

    o Making a list of exciting options shows you're an **Adventurous Leader**. You're not afraid to try new things and encourage others to explore.

    o Thinking of something everyone will enjoy? You're a **Considerate Leader**. You ensure that activities are enjoyable for everyone.

    o Suggesting something new and adventurous? You're a **Pioneering Leader**, always leading the way into exciting new experiences.

- **Kindness Quest:**

    o Offering to show them around highlights your **Empathetic Leadership**. You're kind and understanding, always ready to help.

    o Introducing them to your friends? That's **Inclusive Leadership**. You make sure everyone feels welcome and part of the group.

    o Just a friendly smile? You're a **Supportive Leader**, making sure others feel comfortable and acknowledged in small but meaningful ways.

- Challenge Champion:
  - o Tackling problems head-on shows you're a **Bold Decision-Maker**. You're not afraid to face challenges and take charge.
  - o Asking friends for ideas indicates you're a **Team Collaborator**. You value others' input and excel in working together.
  - o Breaking it down into steps? You're a **Strategic Planner**. You're good at organizing tasks and finding step-by-step solutions.

These qualities can blend and overlap. You might find that you're a bit of an **Empathetic Listener** and a **Creative Thinker** or a **Bold Decision-Maker** with a knack for **Strategic Planning**. Each of these qualities makes you a unique and fantastic leader in your own right!

APPLYING LEADERSHIP SKILLS IN REAL LIFE

Now, it is your chance to turn those leadership skills you've discovered into action! Every day offers new opportunities to use these tools at your home, at school, or out in your community. The idea is to try to make a positive difference, big or small.

ORGANIZING A SCHOOL PROJECT:

- Scenario: Your class has a big project on local history. You can use your leadership skills to help plan the project, divide tasks, and ensure everyone's ideas are heard. As a leader, you'll ensure the project is a fun and educational journey for the whole class.

HELPING IN COMMUNITY EVENTS:

- Scenario: There's a community clean-up day. Use your leadership skills to gather your friends and plan a group effort. Encourage everyone to participate and show how small actions can significantly impact keeping your neighborhood beautiful.

FAMILY SETTINGS:

- **Scenario:** Your family is planning a weekend outing. You can step up and help choose a location, plan the day, and ensure everyone has a role in the outing. It's a great way to show your family how you can lead and make sure everyone has a fun day.

Leadership isn't just for the big moments or to look for applause; you can be a leader in everyday situations, too. Every time you use your skills, you're helping out others and growing stronger as a leader at the same time.

YOUR FIRST LEADERSHIP PROJECT!

Every great leader begins with a first step, and it's your turn now! You don't need to start with something huge and overwhelming. The biggest changes start with the smallest projects, a big heart, and the intention to make a real difference. Think of it as planting a seed that could grow into something bigger.

ACTIVITY: BRAINSTORM YOUR FIRST PROJECT:

Start writing creative ideas. Here's how you can brainstorm a project that's just right for you:

1. Choose Your Interest: Start by picking something you're passionate about. Love reading? How about a book club? Enjoy being outdoors? Maybe a neighborhood clean-up is perfect for you!
2. Make a Plan: Once you've chosen your project, jot down what you'll need to make it happen. Who will you invite? What materials do you need? Where will it take place?
3. Set a Date: Pick a day and time for your project. Make sure it's convenient for everyone who wants to join.
4. Spread the Word: Tell your friends, family, and classmates about your project. The more, the merrier!
5. Lead with Confidence: On the day of your project, remember all the leadership skills you've learned. Be open to everyone's ideas, help where needed, and most importantly, have fun leading your first project!
6. Starting with a small project is a fantastic way to test the waters of leadership. It's not about how big the project is; it's about the passion and effort you put into it. So go ahead and dream up your first project. That would be your contribution to the world.

Trailblazers: Tales of Young Leaders Shaping the World

In this section, we will meet some amazing young girls from around the world who are not just dreaming about making a difference; they are doing it! These are not just any girls; they are young leaders who, like you, have big dreams and even bigger hearts. They're making waves in their communities and beyond, championing causes they believe in, and proving that leadership knows no age.

Anna DeVolld: A Young Guardian of the Bees

First, let's buzz into the world of Anna DeVolld, a young environmentalist from Alaska with a sweet spot for bees. Anna became a bee guardian when she understood these little pollinators' crucial role in our ecosystem, and since then, she's been actively involved in raising awareness about the significance of bees and the dangers they face. Through her efforts, Anna teaches us that even the smallest creatures significantly impact our planet, and it's our job to protect them. Her dedication to bee conservation is a beautiful reminder that caring for nature is a true form of leadership.

Bethany Downer: A Star in Space Communication

Let me introduce Bethany Downer from St. John's, Newfoundland, Canada, whose journey to the stars began as a young girl fascinated by space. Growing up, Bethany's school projects were often centered around space, from asteroids to comets; when she completed her undergraduate degree in geography, Bethany was accepted into the master's program at Space University in Strasbourg, France. Bethany also embarked on an incredible journey with Project PoSSUM, undergoing intensive scientist-astronaut training in Florida. Her training included high-G aerobatic flight and spacesuit training, among other spaceflight preparations. Bethany's story is an awe-inspiring example of how a childhood passion can ignite a path to a career that reaches the stars!

Alondra Fraustro: Young Scientist Turning the Tide for the Environment

Next, let's travel to Monterrey, Mexico, to meet Alondra Fraustro. A young scientist with a big dream: to save our planet. Alondra started "Ciencia Mágica," where she shares her love for science most fantastically through workshops and courses that educate and inspire action for environmental care. She's even been recognized globally for her efforts in creating sustainable communities. Alondra shows us that being a leader means using what you love to make a difference – and that science can be a super tool for change!

REAGAN BISCHOFF: EMPOWERING PEOPLE WITH DISABILITIES

Lastly, let's meet Reagan Bischoff, a young leader from the United States who is passionate about empowering people with disabilities like her. Reagan understands the unique challenges faced by individuals with disabilities and dedicates herself to helping them gain essential skills for independence and confidence. Her work is a powerful testament to the idea that leadership involves understanding, empathy, and the drive to make life better for others.

WRAP-UP

As we close Chapter 6, we reflect on the empowering journey we've embarked upon. From learning to develop essential leadership qualities like confidence, courage, and compassion to mastering ethical decision-making and collaboration, this chapter has been a treasure trove of insights and tools for aspiring young leaders.

We've explored the art of public speaking and celebrated the inspiring stories of young female leaders like Anna DeVolld, Bethany Downer, Alondra Fraustro, and Reagan Bischoff, who have significantly impacted their fields. Their stories are potent examples that leadership is not confined by age but is fueled by passion, integrity, and the courage to make a difference.

Let's carry these lessons and inspirations in our minds, ready to raise our voices and lead with integrity because, remember, every girl has the potential to be a leader, and the journey to discovering and nurturing this starts now.

As we turn the page on this chapter, let me underline that the best skill of being a leader is to learn how to bounce back from tough times. Just like a superhero in a story, a true leader knows how to stand up after a fall, ready to face new challenges with a smile.

This chapter has shown us that even when things get a little tricky, a young leader like you can shine bright because you believe in yourself and know that every mistake is a step toward becoming an even more unique you.

And let's not forget every great leader has a team of cheerleaders supporting them. Just like Anna, Bethany, Alondra, and Reagan, you too can find friends, family, and teachers who believe in your dreams. Together, we can climb higher, laugh louder, and make the world a brighter place.

CHAPTER SEVEN

BE WISE, BE BRAVE: SKILLS FOR SAFETY AND SMART CHOICES

Welcome little wise owls! In this chapter, we're on a mission to equip you with some super-important skills that every girl should know. We'll start by navigating into the essentials of first aid and emergency know-how, where you'll learn how to be calm and confident in tricky situations; next, we'll explore self-defense basics, empowering you to stay safe and feel strong. We'll also journey through the digital world, learning to be innovative and safe online. And finally, we'll master the art of making intelligent choices, helping you to confidently say "yes" or "no" when it matters most. Get ready to learn, grow, and be the brave and wise girl you are meant to be!

FIRST AID AND EMERGENCY KNOW-HOW

Here, we're going to become experts in handling emergencies! We'll start with the basics, like what to do for a scrape or a sprain. It's essential to know how to take care of minor injuries, and we'll learn it step by step.

FIRST AID FUNDAMENTALS.

Scrapes and Cuts: Did you take a tiny tumble? No worries! Here's how to handle it like a pro:

1. Clean the Boo-Boo: First, wash your hands. Then, gently clean the scrape with water. If there's dirt in it, you might need a grown-up's help to clean it out.
2. Put on a Bandage: Dry the area gently and put on a bandage. This keeps it clean and protected.

3. Change the Bandage: If your bandage gets dirty, change it with a new, clean one.
4. Keep an Eye on It: If it's not looking better in a few days or if you see redness and swelling, tell a grown-up.

Sprains and Strains: Ouch! Did you twist something while jumping or running? Here's your quick guide to feeling better:

1. Rest Your Superhero Self: First, stop the activity. Resting the injured part is super important.
2. Ice, Ice: Apply an ice pack wrapped in a textile to the injured area for at least 20 minutes. Do this several times a day to reduce swelling.
3. Elevation is Key: Try to keep the injured part elevated. This helps decrease swelling and pain.
4. Seek Help if Needed: If the pain or swelling doesn't improve, it's time to tell your parents or a grown-up and check in with a healthcare professional.

CALLING FOR HELP:

Sometimes, superheroes need backup, and that's when we call for help! Here is how and when to call 911:

o Know When to Call: 911 is for big emergencies, like if someone is hurt badly, there's a fire, or you need urgent help.
o Stay Calm and Clear: When you call, take a deep breath. Speak calmly and clearly so the operator can understand you.
o Give the Important Details: Tell the operator your name, location, and what happened. They might ask you more questions, so stay on the line and answer as best you can.
o Follow Instructions: The operator might give you instructions. Listen carefully and do as they say.

Remember, calling 911 is a big responsibility, and you can do it! Just stay calm, and help will be on its way.

BIG EMERGENCY SITUATIONS:

In case of big emergencies like a fire or an earthquake, knowing what to do is super important. Allow me to show you the essentials:

In Case of a Fire:

- o If you see smoke or flames, yell for help, get out of the building as quickly and safely as possible, and call 911.
- o Stop it, drop it, and roll yourself in case your clothes catch fire.
- o Don't hide; firefighters are here to help you.

During an Earthquake:

- o Find a safe spot away from windows, like under a sturdy table.
- o Drop, Cover, and Hold On until the earthquake stops.
- o Once it's safe, move to an open area away from buildings.
- o Staying calm and knowing these steps can make a big difference in an emergency.

- Note: Different regions and countries may face various emergencies, like hurricanes, cyclones, etc. It's crucial to know the types of emergencies that can happen in your area. Always remember to follow basic safety steps and listen to instructions from authorities; they will guide you on what to do, whether it's to evacuate or stay safe indoors. Being prepared and informed is a super skill in any emergency!
- Important Reminder: In case of big emergencies, always look for guidance from your parents, guardians, or another responsible adult. It's essential not to act alone, and they can help you understand the situation better and decide the safest course of action. Teamwork is key in handling any emergency situation safely and effectively!

SELF-DEFENSE BASICS: STAY SAFE, FEEL STRONG:

In this section, we will learn key skills to help you protect yourself and be prepared for different situations. You'll learn the importance of being aware of your surroundings, standing strong and balanced, and mastering simple but effective self-defense moves. This section empowers you to feel secure in different situations. So, let's start this important journey of learning how to stay safe and feel strong!

AWARENESS IS YOUR FIRST SHIELD

Understanding your surroundings is like having a built-in safety radar that helps you notice where you are and who is around you. When you are walking home from school, playing in the park, or shopping at the mall, keeping an eye on your surroundings helps you stay safe. This means not getting too absorbed in your phone or music; instead, look around, listen, and stay alert. This way, you can spot anything unusual and know when to seek help or move to a safer place. It's smart, simple, and one of the best ways to protect yourself.

STRONG STANCE, STRONG YOU:

A strong stance is like the solid foundation of a house. Meaning that it keeps you steady and prepared. This strong stance is for self-defense, and it is also a powerful way to walk through life ready for whatever comes your way.

To practice a firm stance, you'll need to:

- o Plant Your Feet: Stand with your feet shoulder-width apart. This gives you a stable base.
- o Bend Your Knees Slightly: Keep your knees a little bent, not locked. This makes it easier to move quickly if needed.
- o Keep Your Body-Centered: Align your body so you're facing forward, ready to move in any direction.
- o Head Held High: Keep your head up and look straight ahead. This shows confidence and helps you stay alert.

SIMPLE MOVES FOR SAFETY

Here, I will show you simple yet smart self-defense moves that are easy to remember and can really make a difference when you need to stand up for yourself. These moves are not about strength; you need to be smart and swift to use them.

- o **The Palm Strike:** Imagine pushing open a heavy door; that's how you do a palm strike with your palm open. If someone's too close, use the base of your palm to push them away gently.
- o **The Elbow Jab:** If someone sneaks up behind you, an elbow jab can help. It's like a quick backward poke with your elbow.

94

- The Knee Lift: If someone is too close in front of you, a quick knee lift to the shin can be effective. It's like doing a high knee exercise in gym class, fast and direct.
- The Stomp and Run: If someone grabs you, stomp hard on your foot. It might surprise them enough so you can run to a safe place.
- The Loud Whistle: Sometimes, the best defense is drawing attention. Carrying a whistle and blowing it loudly or just screaming can alert others around you that you need help.

> Note: Remember, these techniques are for self-defense purposes only and should be used responsibly just to keep you safe. Practicing them will help you feel more confident and prepared.

ESSENTIAL REMINDERS TO STAY SAFE

- Seek Help if Threatened: If you feel threatened, it's always okay to look for help. Tell your parents or a trusted adult if the situation isn't urgent. But if it's an emergency, don't hesitate to call the police or use 911.
- Stay in Safe Places: Never accept an offer to enter a car or house without your parents' permission, especially a stranger, even if they say they want to help you. It's always safer to stay in public areas with other people around.
- Trust Your Instincts: If something doesn't feel right, it probably isn't. Trust your feelings, seek help, or leave the situation if possible.
- Make Noise: If you're in a situation where you feel unsafe, don't be afraid to shout or make noise to attract attention.
- Have Emergency Contacts: Always have a list of emergency contacts memorized or stored in your phone; be sure to include your parents, relatives, or a family friend.

> Note: Remember, your safety is the most important thing. Being prepared and aware of these tips will help you stay safe in different situations.

NAVIGATING THE DIGITAL WORLD: SMART AND SAFE ONLINE

And now, we'll become internet-savvy explorers, learning the ropes of how to journey through the online world confidently and safely. This thrilling adventure will take us through understanding our digital footprints and how they reflect our online actions, just like the unique sparkles we leave behind. Also, we'll unlock the secrets of safe sharing, keeping our personal information private while enjoying the vast, exciting digital landscape.

In our map, we have also learned how to tackle cyberbullying with courage and intelligent strategies, ensuring we stand strong and kind in the face of online challenges. We'll become pros at surfing the net, discovering how to spot safe spaces, and steering clear of risky online waters. And now, buckle up, tech-savvy girls, because it's time to embark on a journey of becoming digital citizens in this vast, amazing online universe!

DIGITAL FOOTPRINT FUN

Did you know you leave a digital footprint whenever you post, like, or share something online? As if you were leaving sparkly glitter trails wherever you go on the internet. So, let's make sure our glitter is the good kind!

- o Think Before You Click: Every post or picture adds to your digital footprint. Ask yourself, "Is this something I'd be happy for everyone to see?"
- o Privacy is Key: Keep personal info like your home address, school name, or phone number private. It's like a secret treasure that's just for you and your family.
- o Be a Positive Poster: Share fun, kind, and positive stuff. Your digital footprint should show how cool and incredible you are!
- o Let's make our digital footprints something to be proud of, shining bright and safe online!

SHARING WITH CARE

Navigating what to share online can be like solving a secret message where you need a code. Let's crack the code together:

- Your Personal Info is Like a Hidden Treasure: As we saw before, keep your full name, address, phone number, and school details a secret. It's special info meant just for you and your family.
- Photos: Share photos that are fun and friendly. But remember, some pictures, like those showing your house or school, are best kept private.
- Think 'Feel-Good' Sharing: Share stuff that makes you and others feel good – like your art, achievements, or fun experiences.
- Ask for the Green Light: Not sure if it's okay to post something? Ask a parent or guardian. They're like your co-pilots in the digital world!
- Sharing with care keeps you and your friends smiling online!

BEAT CYBERBULLYING

Here's how we can beat cyberbullying.:
- Spot the Signs: If someone is being hurtful or mean to you or a friend online, that's cyberbullying. It could be rude messages, posts, or even sharing personal info without permission.
- Speak Up: Tell your parents or a trusted adult about what's happening. They can help you figure out the best steps to take.
- Stay Strong and Kind: Remember, their words reflect on them, not you. Stay positive and don't sink to their level.
- Block and Report: Most apps and sites let you block users and report bullying. Use these tools to keep your space safe.

> IMPORTANT!
> If someone online (or in the real world) asks you not to tell your parents, that's a big warning signal. You should always feel comfortable talking to your parents or a trusted adult about anything that happens. And if someone threatens to harm you or anyone else, don't believe them, and don't keep it a secret. Go straight to your parents, a trusted adult, or even the police. Your safety is the most important, and there are people who will help you.

Are you starting to surf the net? Do it right. With these tips, you will become a pro at picking safe websites and steering clear of the sketchy ones. Here's how we do it:

- Look for the Padlock: Safe websites often have a little padlock symbol in the address bar. It's like a secret code that says, "This site is secure!"
- Be a Web Address Detective: Keep an eye on web addresses. If something looks a bit off, like a weird spelling, it might be a sneaky, unsafe site.
- Smart Clicks Only: See a strange link or a too-good-to-be-true offer? Let's skip those! Only click on things that look safe and sound.
- Trusty Sites are Besties: Stick with websites you and your family know and love. They're like your online BFFs; they're always there and super reliable.
- Parent Power: Always remember your parents are your best allies in navigating the online world. If you're unsure about a website or something you see online, talk to them. Trusting your parents and working together makes browsing safer and a lot more fun!

With these terrific tips, you can surf smart and have a blast online!

SAY YES TO NO:

Ready for a superpower that's going to change your world? It's called "**Say YES to NO!**" Sometimes, the most incredible, bravest thing you can do is say "NO." It's not a magic spell to skip chores, dodge homework, or zoom past school responsibilities. Nope, this power is for something way more important: your safety and feelings. When something doesn't feel right, or you're in a situation that seems wrong, even with an adult or someone in charge, that's your moment to stand tall and say "NO."

We will dive into why saying "NO" is actually saying "YES" to yourself and your safety. If you ever feel unsafe or in danger, it's super important to talk to your parents, a trusted adult, or even the police. Your safety is a big deal, and saying "NO" is one of your mightiest tools to protect it. Use your "NO" for good to keep yourself safe and sound in this big adventure called life!

DECISION DETECTIVE

Ready to put on your detective hat? As Decision Detectives, we'll hunt for clues to make good choices in our daily lives.

- o Clue Hunt: Every decision, big or small, has clues. Need to choose a snack? Look for clues like nutrition and taste. Need to choose an after-school activity? Will it be art class or soccer practice? Think about what each activity involves. What do you enjoy more, being creative or being active?
- o Weigh the Evidence: Just like a detective weighs evidence, think about the pros and cons of each choice.
- o Solving the Puzzle: Put together your clues to make a decision that feels right.

Bigger decisions might seem tricky, but we can figure out the best choice with our detective skills!

ASSERTIVENESS ADVENTURES

Being assertive is learning to say what you think at the moment you need it most in a reasonable manner. Here's how to steer confidently:

- o Voice Your Choice: Whether it's picking a game to play or sharing your opinion in class, remember, your voice matters.
- o Yes or No with Confidence: It's okay to say "no" to things you're not feeling safe with and "yes" to things you love. Practice speaking both with confidence.
- o Express Confidently: Share what you think and feel honestly. If something makes you happy, say it! If something bothers you, it's okay to speak up.

You are the captain, and you have your own compass to show you the way. Saying YES or NO with assertiveness is a skill that will help you for the rest of your life.

TRUST YOUR GUT

Sometimes, the world can be a bit like a maze, full of twists and turns, and you have a built-in compass: your instincts! They help you navigate the world, showing you when to take a step forward or when to say "No" and take a different path. If something, some decision, or a moment doesn't feel right, trust yourself!

Remember, every "No" you say when something feels off is actually a big "Yes" to you and your safety. You're the boss of your journey, and listening to your gut helps you be the bravest, most brilliant, and most fantastic version of yourself!

WRAP-UP

Wow, what a journey we've had in Chapter 7! We've explored some fundamental skills every girl needs to know to be safe and make wise choices. Let's take a moment to remember the key things we've learned:

- **First Aid and Emergency** Know-How: We've become confident handling minor injuries and learned when to ask for help. Remember, knowing what to do makes a big difference, whether a scrape or a sprain.

- **Big Emergency Situations:** From fires to earthquakes, we now know the essential steps to stay safe. Remember, understanding what to do in these situations can help keep you and others safe.
- **Self-Defense Basics:** We've discovered how to be aware of our surroundings, stand firm, and learn simple self-defense moves. These skills are about feeling safe and confident, no matter where you are.
- **Navigating the Digital World:** Our online adventure taught us to be smart and safe while exploring the vast digital universe. From managing our digital footprint to tackling cyberbullying, we're now savvy and secure digital citizens.
- **Say YES to NO:** We've mastered the art of making decisions, learning when to say "no" and how to do it confidently. Every choice you make is a step towards being the amazing girl you are.

o

Being wise and brave isn't knowing all things but learning when and how to use your knowledge to make the best choices for yourself in different situations. Whether dealing with a scraped knee, standing up for yourself, or making smart choices online, now you have the skills to handle it all.

You're growing into a wise, brave, and intelligent girl, ready to take on the world with confidence and care. So, keep these lessons close to your heart, and remember, you're always stronger than you think!

CHAPTER EIGHT

LIFE LESSONS

Join me on an exciting journey in our "Life Lessons" chapter! Here, we will discover some amazing things about the world and ourselves because this chapter will be similar to an adventure map, guiding you through the treasures of understanding democracy, the art of asking intelligent questions (the Socratic Method), the endless joy of learning, and the big world of global issues. Don't worry; we will explore these big ideas in fun and easy ways where you can become a mini-expert on some crucial stuff, learn new ways of relating to the world, and, the best part, guess what? You'll have lots of fun along the way. Here starts a new adventure full of curiosity and excitement!

TOGETHER WE DECIDE: A DEMOCRACY ADVENTURE

Have you ever wondered what it means to live in a democracy? It's like being part of a team where everyone gets a say in the decisions. Of course, it is related to big elections and governments, but it is also something we live in daily, even in our family matters.

In society, as in every team, we make choices together, and each person's opinion is essential. The best part is that you can practice democracy right in your own home, just like Aysel and Shani do! Let me share a little story about them to illustrate the beauty of democracy and participation in our everyday lives.

When Aysel and Shani have different ideas about what movie to watch or what game to play, we use something that's a big part of democracy: voting this way, everyone in our family gets their say, and all voices are valued.

For instance, there was a time when Aysel was all set for a laugh-out-loud cartoon while Shani was enchanted by the idea of a fairy tale movie. To find out which movie to watch, we voted, meaning that each of us raised a hand for the movie we wanted to see. The fairy tale movie won that evening, but the most crucial part was that Aysel knew her choice was considered. That's the essence of democracy: everyone's opinion counts.

In our family, voting on things like movie nights or which board game to play is a fun way to show how every family member's opinion is important; it teaches Aysel and Shani that even when your choice isn't the winner, being part of the decision-making process is what truly matters.

Try to remember our little voting ritual next time you find yourself in a situation with friends or family where a choice needs to be made. Use your voice and vote, just like Aysel and Shani. And explain that It's not about the final selection but about participating and making decisions together when the real magic of democracy and participation starts!

CURIOSITY QUEST: EXPLORING THE WORLD THROUGH QUESTIONS

Have you ever wondered why the sky is blue or why we have different seasons? Questions like these are the start of a fantastic adventure we called "Curiosity Quest." It's all about exploring the world by asking questions, just like a famous philosopher named Socrates did a long, long time ago. He believed that asking questions was the best way to learn and understand the world better.

Let me share a great evening with Aysel and Shani, which turned into a fantastic space exploration. It all started when Aysel asked, "Why is the sun so hot? Instead of providing a direct answer, I encouraged her to think, asking, 'What do you think makes the sun different from other stars?" This sparked a light in her eyes as she began to hypothesize, suggesting maybe it's because it's closer to us.

Then Shani asked with boundless curiosity, "Does the sun ever take a break at night?" This led us to explore how the sun is always shining, even when it's night for us. We discussed the Earth's rotation and how it creates day and night.

"But why do stars twinkle?" Aysel wondered next, looking at the night sky from our window. We delved into how light travels from distant stars and how the Earth's atmosphere makes them appear to twinkle.

Our living room transformed into a spaceship of imagination, journeying through questions about the sun, stars, and the vast universe. We talked about how stars are like giant balls of gas burning and how the sun is our closest star, giving us light and warmth. Each question led to more reading, exploring, and learning together. We talked about astronauts, the solar system, and even the possibility of life on other planets.

You can start your own Curiosity Quest with friends or family. Next time you're curious about something, ask more questions about it instead of looking for the answer right away. For example:

o If you see a beautiful flower, ask, "Why does it have that color?" Or "Why does it have more or less petals than others?"
o When you see a bird flying, wonder, "How do they know where to go when they migrate?"

In the grown-up world, this is called **"the Socratic Method"**; every question you ask opens up a new world of ideas and possibilities. This way of asking and thinking helps you become a super-intelligent problem-solver and a creative thinker.

Are you ready to start your own Curiosity Quest? Remember, every question is a star waiting to be discovered in the vast sky of knowledge.

Step 1: Become a Question Explorer

o Find a notebook or create a special section in your journal. This Will be your "Curiosity Quest Journal."
o Set a goal to ask at least three "why" or "how" questions each day about anything that sparks your interest.

Step 2: Start with What's Around You

- o Look around your home, school, or neighborhood. Choose one thing you see every day but haven't thought much about. It could be a plant, an old building, a pet, or even a kitchen appliance.
- o Ask questions about it: "Why does it look like that?" "How does it work?" "What is its purpose?"

Step 3: Investigate and Discover

- o For each question, do a little research. You could ask an adult, look it up in a book or a safe online source, or even make observations on your own.
- o Write down the answers you find in your Curiosity Quest Journal.

Step 4: Share Your Discoveries

- o At the end of the week, share what you've learned with your family or friends. You could make it a fun presentation or a casual conversation during dinner.
- o Discussing your findings can lead to even more questions and discoveries!

Step 5: Reflect and Repeat

- o At the end of each Curiosity Quest, reflect on what you learned and how it made you feel. Did you discover something surprising or exciting?

Start a new quest each week or whenever you're ready for another adventure in learning.

A WORLD OF WONDERS: A LIFELONG JOURNEY OF LEARNING

Education is not only what happens in school, but it is an amazing journey that lasts your whole life. Let's think about all the different ways we learn. Sure, there's reading, writing, and math in school, but learning is much more. For instance, we learn from our grandparents' stories, our experiments in our backyard, and even the games we play with our friends.

Even as a grown-up, I am constantly amazed by how much there is to learn and understand about the world. Every case I study, every law I analyze, and every political event I witness teaches me something new. It is this continuous learning that keeps my work exciting and fulfilling.

As a political scientist, I've delved into the complex world of politics and governance, discovering new perspectives and ideas with each study. And here's the secret: no matter how much you learn, there's always more. The world is filled with mysteries and wonders waiting to be explored. Even now, I'm still struck by the beauty and complexity of how things work and how much is out there that we don't know yet.

I remember when Aysel and Shani learned to ride bikes. That was learning, too! They fell a few times, but each time they got back up, they learned to balance and pedal a little better; in the end, every scrape was a lesson in persistence and courage. This learning journey goes to gaining knowledge but also to keeping our capacity to be astounded. The real magic is when you start asking questions and staying open to new ideas, regardless of age.

I want to inspire you, just like I've been inspired, to be a lifelong learner; every day is an opportunity to learn something new, to be amazed, and to grow. Whether through books, people travel, or hobbies, keep exploring, questioning, and keeping the wonder alive.

MY LIFELONG LEARNING PASSPORT: YOUR JOURNEY OF DISCOVERY

- **Passport Creation:**
  - Make your own "Lifelong Learning Passport". You can use a small notebook or make one with paper and decorations. This passport will be a record of your learning adventures.

- **Collect Stamps:**
  - For every new thing you learn, stick a stamp on your passport.
  - Example: Read a book about planets. Stick a "Books and Stories" as your stamp. Learned a new word in a different language? Sick a "Skills Stamp" on your passport.

- **Categories of Learning:**
  - **Exploration Stamp:** This is for all your adventures, big or small. Whether you're visiting a new place, a museum, or a historical place, every discovery earns you an Exploration Stamp.
  - **Skills Stamp:** Got a new skill? Fantastic! Whether baking cookies, riding a bike, or learning to swim, add a Skills Stamp to celebrate.
  - **Books and Stories Stamp:** Are you a bookworm? For every book you read, add a Books and Stories Stamp. It can be about princesses, space adventures, or mysterious mysteries; all books are awesome!

- **Curiosity Questions Stamp:** Every time you ask a question and find the answer, it deserves a stamp. What did you learn?
- **Creative Artist Stamp:** Love drawing, painting, or making crafts? Every time you create something, you earn a Creative Artist Stamp. Let your imagination soar!
- **Tech Whiz Stamp:** For all the tech-savvy girls out there! If you learn something new about computer apps, or even if you help someone with a tech problem, you get a Tech Whiz Stamp.
- **Global Explorer Stamp:** Learn something about a different country or culture. That's awesome! Add a Global Explorer Stamp to your passport for each new place or culture you discover.
- **Community Connector Stamp:** This one is for helping out in your community. Whether volunteering, participating in a community project, or learning about important social issues, you get a Community Connector Stamp.

Exploration Stamps

Skills Stamps

Books and Stories Stamps

Curiosity Questions Stamp

Creativity Artist Stamps

Tech Whiz Stamps

Global Explorer Stamps

Community Connector Stamps

- Share Your Adventures:
  - At the end of each month, share your passport with your family or friends. Tell them about your stamps and what each one represents. Discussing your learning adventures can inspire others and give you ideas for collecting new stamps.

- **Reflect and Dream:**
  - At the end of the year, look back at all the stamps you've collected. How have they shaped your understanding and interests? Dream about what stamps you want to collect next year. What new things do you want to explore and learn?

SMALL HANDS, BIG IMPACT

Now, we're going on an adventure to understand some big things happening around our planet. These are called "global issues". While they might sound serious, don't worry; we will explore them in a way that's just right for you.

Global issues are significant challenges that affect people and places all over the world. Such as caring for our environment, helping people in need, and ensuring everyone is treated fairly and kindly. Knowing about these issues is crucial because even though you are young, you can make a huge difference!

Let's start with the environment. Our beautiful planet needs our help to stay healthy and happy. Pollution and gas emissions have changed the world's climate, creating more and more droughts and hurricanes. The use of plastics everywhere has created a massive problem of plastic soups in our oceans, threatening sea creatures.

Simple actions like recycling, saving water, and planting trees are ways to show love for our Earth. When Aysel and Shani recycle plastic bags or bottles, we talk about how our actions impact our Earth and how we can make positive impacts with small actions!

Another critical issue is helping others. There are people in the world who might not have everything they need, like food, water, or a safe place to live. We can show kindness by donating money or clothes we've outgrown, sharing our toys, or even being a friend to someone who feels alone.

Lastly, treating everyone with respect and kindness is a big part of improving the world. This means understanding and celebrating what makes each person unique, like where they're from, what they believe, or how they see the world. Remember, every person is special, just like you!

Now, you might be thinking, "Can I really make a difference?" Absolutely, yes! Every small action adds up to big changes. When we do our part, we can make our world happier, safer, and more loving. So, let's be curious, kind, and ready to help. With tiny hands and big hearts, we can be heroes for our planet and its people. What small action will you take today to make a significant impact?"

GLOBAL GUARDIAN QUIZ: HOW CAN YOU MAKE A DIFFERENCE?

1. What do you do when you see a piece of trash on the ground at the park?

    A. Pick it up and throw it in the trash can.
    B. Leave it there; it's not mine.
    C. Tell an adult or a park worker about it.

2. What can you do to save water at home?

    A. Take shorter showers.
    B. Leave the water running while brushing my teeth.
    C. Water the plants every day.

3. If you have toys or clothes you don't use anymore, what's a good thing to do with them?

    A. Keep them in my closet; I might need them one day.
    B. Throw them away.
    C. Donate them to someone who needs them.

4. Why is it important to learn about people from different places?

    A. To understand and appreciate everyone's uniqueness.
    B. It's not important.
    C. I can visit them one day.

5. What is one way you can be kind to others at school?

    A. By helping someone who is struggling with their work.
    B. By only playing with my best friends.
    C. By keeping all my snacks to myself.

Answers:
- Mostly A's: You're a Super Global Guardian! You understand the importance of taking care of our planet and people.
- Mostly B's: There's more you can learn about being a Global Guardian. Every small action can make a big difference!
- Mostly C's: Great effort! You're on your way to becoming a Global Guardian. Keep

WRAP-UP

As we close this chapter, let's take a moment to reflect on the incredible journey we've just been on. We've explored some big ideas like democracy, the art of questioning, and global challenges, and we've done it in ways that are engaging and totally doable for young adventurers like you!

DEMOCRACY IN ACTION: A FAMILY AFFAIR

We've seen how democracy isn't just for politicians; it's for everyone, including you! Just like Aysel and Shani, you've learned how every voice matters and how making decisions together can be both fun and important. Remember, your opinion counts, whether you're choosing a movie or helping decide family activities.

CURIOSITY QUEST: THE ADVENTURE OF ASKING

Our journey through the world of questions has shown us that curiosity is your superpower. Asking "why" and "how" is more than just seeking answers; it's about opening doors to new worlds and possibilities. You've taken the first steps to becoming a great thinker and problem solver, just like the ancient philosophers.

Making a Difference: Small Hands, Big Impact

Understanding global issues might seem overwhelming, but you've learned that even the smallest actions can make a big difference. From recycling to showing kindness to others, you're already on your way to making our planet a better place. Your actions, no matter how small, are powerful.

Looking Ahead: Lifelong Learning and Beyond

Learning doesn't stop here. Every day is a new opportunity to discover something unique, ask a new question, or make a positive impact. So keep your curiosity alive, stay engaged with the world around you, and continue to be the fantastic, thoughtful, and caring person you are.

As we turn the page on this chapter, I encourage you to carry these lessons with you. Be brave, be curious, and be kind. You have the power to create change, and your journey is just beginning. Let's keep learning and growing together!

CHAPTER NINE

ADVENTURES AND EXPLORATION

Hey there, awesome adventurers! Get ready to strap on your explorer hats and dive into a thrilling space of discovery and fun! This chapter will lead us through exciting skills and extraordinary activities that are all about making our own adventures.

Imagine setting up your tent like a camping pro, navigating outdoors with just a compass, and cracking secret codes like a real-life spy. We're not just stopping there; we'll be detectives uncovering historical mysteries, stargazers unraveling the secrets of the night sky, and creative geniuses crafting our own epic adventure tales. This chapter celebrates every girl's fearless, curious, and ingenious spirit. Then, lace up your adventure shoes, and let's jump into a journey where every girl is the hero of her own exciting story. Let the adventure begin!

CAMPING AND OUTDOOR SKILLS

Are you ready to become the ultimate camping champion? This section is all about mastering the most astounding camping skills that will turn you into a nature-loving superstar.

SETTING UP A TENT

Setting up a tent is like building a secret fort; it's exciting and super fun! This activity is more than just a practical skill; it teaches patience, problem-solving, and teamwork. I remember the first time my friends and I attempted to set up our tent. The poles seemed to have a mind of their own, and the fabric appeared too vast. But with determination and a bit of guidance, we transformed those flapping sheets into a cozy shelter. Here's how to do it:

1. Find the Perfect Spot: Look for a flat, dry area. Avoid places under trees (watch out for falling branches!) or at the bottom of hills (hello, surprise water slide if it rains!).
2. Lay Out Your Tent: Spread your tent on the ground. This is like laying out a giant puzzle on the floor.
3. Assemble the Poles: Connect the poles; they usually snap together like magic wands!
4. Raise the Tent: Now, the fun part! Get the poles through the tent's sleeves and watch your tent come to life. It's like waving a magic wand and seeing your castle appear!
5. Secure It: Hammer those stakes into the ground to keep your tent from flying away like a giant kite.
6. Final Touches: Add the rainfly for extra protection – it's like a tent's superhero cape against rain!

OUTDOOR COOKING ADVENTURES

There's something magical about cooking over a campfire because it's not just the food but the experience over the fire. Outdoor cooking is a delightful way to foster independence and an adventurous spirit. Aysel and Shani loved the sense of accomplishment they felt when they first cooked outdoors. It was sausages and roasted marshmallows, but it tasted like a gourmet feast to them because they had made it themselves. Here are two simple and yummy recipes to try:

Campfire Roasted Sausages:

1. Safety First: Always have an adult around when you're near the fire. Safety is the number one rule in the wild!
2. Get Your Sausages Ready: Grab some yummy sausages. Any kind you love!
3. Skewer Them Up: Carefully put each sausage on a skewer or a clean, long stick. It's like preparing your magic wand for a delicious spell!
4. Roasting Time: Hold your sausage skewer over the campfire. Not too close; we don't want them to become charcoal sticks! Turn them slowly so they cook evenly. It's like giving them a mini sunbath!
5. Enjoy: Once they're nicely browned and sizzling, let them cool a bit, then enjoy your tasty, smoky treat!

Marshmallow Magic:

What's a campfire without marshmallows, right?

1. Safety First: Always have an adult around when you're near the fire. Safety is our number one rule in the wild.
2. Marshmallow Time: Get some fluffy marshmallows ready.
3. Skewer and Roast: Like the sausages, skew your marshmallows and roast them over the campfire. Watch them get golden brown; it's like watching clouds turn into little golden pillows!
4. The Perfect Roast: Some like them lightly toasted, and some love them super gooey. Roast them to your liking!
5. Sandwich It: For extra yumminess, sandwich your marshmallow using two graham crackers with a piece of chocolate. It's a campfire classic: the legendary s'more!

The best part of outdoor cooking is enjoying your food under the stars, surrounded by nature's beauty and your loved ones. Enjoy the cooking, the eating, and the whole adventure of making it!

NATURE SCAVENGER HUNTS

Alright, adventure team! You've mastered setting up your tent and have become pros at campfire cooking. Now, let's amp up the fun with a Nature Scavenger Hunt! This is not like any other hunt, but a super cool mission to explore and learn about the natural world around us.

Organizing Your Scavenger Hunt:

1. Safety First: Before starting, have an adult check the area to ensure it's safe for exploration. Avoid areas with steep hills, deep water, or dense woods.
2. Stay Hydrated and Protected: Bring water, wear sunscreen, and dress appropriately for the weather. It's like gearing up for a mini-adventure!

3. Make a List: Write a list of things to find or tasks to complete. Think colorful leaves, smooth pebbles, different types of flowers, or even sounds you might hear in nature, like a bird's song or the rustle of leaves.
4. Buddy Up: Always stick with a buddy or in a group. It's like having your own adventure squad; plus, it's safer and way more fun!
5. Set Boundaries: Make sure everyone knows the safe area for the hunt. It's like marking your playground in the wild. It's essential to stay within sight and shouting distance of the adults in charge.
6. Ready, Set, Go!: Start the hunt with a big cheer! Remember, it's not just about finding things quickly; it's about enjoying the search and discovering the beauty around you.
7. Document Your Finds: Bring a camera or use a phone (with permission!) to snap pictures of your finds. It's like being a nature detective collecting evidence.
8. Check-In Regularly: If the scavenger hunt area is large, set times to check in with the adults or regroup. This way, everyone stays connected and safe.
9. Share Your Discoveries: Once everyone's back, share what you found. It's super fun to see the different things each team discovered and learned.

> Respect Nature: Remember, while we're out exploring, we must respect nature. That means no picking flowers or disturbing wildlife. It's about finding joy in observing and leaving everything just as you found it for others to enjoy, too.

A Nature Scavenger Hunt is a game and an adventure into the heart of the natural world where we can connect with nature, learn new things, and make incredible memories. Therefore, get ready to start your scavenger hunt and see what amazing things you can find. And let the adventure continue!

COMPASS QUEST: MASTERING THE ART OF ORIENTEERING

After rocking the scavenger hunt, are you ready for your next fabulous adventure? It's time to become a navigation ninja with some basic orientation and compass skills. This is your ticket to becoming a self-reliant, direction-finding superstar!

BECOMING A COMPASS WHIZ:

- Meet Your Compass: A compass has a magnetic needle that always points north. The compass housing is the round part that turns, marked with directions: North (N), South (S), East (E), and West (W). The travel arrow's direction on the base of the compass shows where you're going.
- Understanding the Basics: Learn the compass basics: the needle, the dial, and the directions. It's like unlocking a secret code to the world's map!
- Holding It Properly: To use a compass correctly, hold it flat in your hand at chest level. Make sure it's level so the needle can move freely.
- Finding North: Look at the needle: one end is usually marked or colored differently. This end points North. Rotate your whole body while keeping the compass level until the marked end of the needle lines up with the 'N' on the compass housing.

ORIENTEERING ADVENTURES:

- Stay Safe: When outdoors, always orienteer with a buddy or in a group, and let an adult know your course. Safety is our number one rule in the wild!
- Set Up a Course: Create a simple orienteering course in a safe area. Use landmarks like a big tree or a bench as points to find. Decide which direction you want to travel. Turn the compass housing so that the direction (like "E" for East) lines up with the direction of the travel arrow. Keeping the compass level, turn your body until the marked end of the needle lines up with "N" in the housing. The direction of the travel arrow now points in the direction you want to go.
- Using Landmarks: Pick a landmark in the direction of the arrow points and walk towards it. Periodically check the compass to ensure you're still going in the right direction.
- Use Your Compass and Map: Now, use your compass and map to navigate to these points. It's like being on a treasure hunt, where the treasure is the joy of finding your way!
- Learn as You Go: As you navigate, observe how the landscape changes. You'll start to see how the map reflects real life; it's like having an X-ray vision of the Earth!

Remember:

o Stay in Known Areas: When you're just starting, practice using your compass in familiar areas. Avoid exploring places that are too remote or challenging.
o Always Have a Buddy: Orienteering is more fun and much safer when you do it with someone else. Whether it's a friend, a sibling, or an adult, having a buddy means you've got each other's backs.

- o Let someone know: Always tell an adult where you're going and what your orienteering plan is. It's like leaving a trail of breadcrumbs so someone can find you if needed.
- o Bring Essentials: Along with your compass and map, carry a small backpack with essentials like water, a snack, a whistle, and a small first-aid kit. It's like having a mini survival kit for your adventure.
- o Check the Weather: Ensure the weather before heading out. It's not much fun orienteering in bad weather and can be unsafe.
- o Know Your Limits: It's great to challenge yourself, but you also need to know when it's time to take a break or head back. Listening to your body is a super important skill for any adventurer.

Safety, as you now know, is super important in all outdoor activities, and orienteering is no exception. By following these tips, you can enjoy your compass adventures to the fullest, knowing you're taking good care of yourself and the world. Happy orienteering!

WHY ORIENTEERING ROCKS

Orienteering is more than finding your way; you can build other skills, such as problem-solving and self-esteem, all by connecting with the environment. It teaches you to trust your skills and be self-reliant, which is super important for any adventurer!

Are you ready to step into the shoes of a navigation expert? Grab your compass, unfold your map, and let's get orienteering! Who knows what unique places you'll discover?

CODE BREAKERS: SECRETS OF CRYPTOGRAPHY

Alright, secret agents! After mastering the art of orienteering, it's time to enter into the mysterious and exciting world of hidden messages and basic cryptography. This is where you become code-cracking experts, unlocking the secrets of languages and coding!

CRYPTOGRAPHY: A SECRET JOURNEY THROUGH TIME

Here we are in the fascinating world of cryptography, a realm where secret messages have been hidden in plain sight for centuries! Imagine being a spy in ancient times or a codebreaker in a world war; that's how fascinating the history of cryptography is.

- o **Ancient Beginnings:** Our journey starts in ancient Egypt, where hieroglyphs were sometimes used to hide secret messages. Fast forward to ancient Greece, and meet the Spartans with their Scytale, a tool for sending private battle messages. It was like a magical wand that only revealed its secrets when wrapped around a special rod!
- o **The Caesar Cipher:** Next, we zoom into Julius Caesar's time. He used a simple but clever cipher for his confidential messages, shifting each letter in the alphabet a few steps down. Imagine writing a secret note that could only be read by those who knew the notable shift!
- o **The Enigma of World War II:** Fast forward to the 20th century, where cryptography played a huge role in World War II. The Germans used the Enigma machine, a complex device that seemed unbreakable. But thanks to brilliant minds like Alan Turing, the Allies cracked the code, a turning point in the war.
- o **Modern Cryptography:** Today, cryptography is everywhere in the digital world. It protects our online messages, secures transactions, and keeps our digital lives safe. It's like having an invisible superhero guarding our secrets!

There you have it, a tour of the secret, thrilling world of cryptography. From ancient rods to digital codes, it's a journey that shows just how intelligent and creative humans can be when it comes to keeping secrets. Now, it is your turn to start your own secret code adventure!

THE SECRET CODE CHALLENGE

Decode the secret messages using the cipher you will create, solve the riddles, or complete the tasks.

Materials Needed:

- o A set of secret messages (riddles or simple tasks) encoded using a basic cipher.
- o A cipher key for decoding the messages.
- o Players need a pen and paper to write down their decoded messages and answers.

Setup:

- o **Create the Cipher:** Use a substitution code. Each letter in the alphabet is replaced with a number or symbol. For instance, an A will be 1, a B will be 2, a C will be 3, and so on, as I show you below.

A	B	C	D	E	F	G	H	I	J	K	L	M	N
1	2	3	4	5	6	7	8	9	10	11	12	13	14
O	P	Q	R	S	T	R	U	V	W	X	Y	Z	
15	16	17	18	19	20	21	22	23	24	25	26	27	

- o **Prepare Secret Messages:** Write a series of riddles or simple tasks in plain text, then encode them using your cipher. For example, a riddle like "What has keys but can't open locks?" becomes encoded with your cipher. If you want to write a message like "Hello Aysel," you will write "8 5 12 12 15 - 1 26 19 5 12", being the 8=H, the 5=E, the 12=L, and so on.
- o **Print or Display the Cipher** Key: This key will help players decode the messages. It should show the substitution for each letter.

How to Play:

1. Decode the Message: Players use the cipher key to decode the secret messages.
2. Solve the Riddle or Complete the Task: Once decoded, each message reveals a riddle to solve or a simple task to complete. For example, the riddle above, when decoded, should read, "What has keys but can't open locks?" (Answer: A piano).
3. Keep Score: Players earn points for each correctly decoded message and solve the riddle or completed task.
4. Winner: At the end of the game, the player with the most points wins.

Variations for More Fun:

- o **Time Challenge:** Set a time limit for decoding each message to add excitement.
- o **Team Play:** Players can form teams to solve the codes and riddles together.

- o **Create Your Code:** Encourage players to create coded messages for others to decode.

Create your own Scytale and use it to encode and decode secret messages. You can use this with your sister or your friends!

Materials Needed:
- o A cylindrical object (like a rolling pin or a thick marker)
- o A strip of paper (long enough to wrap around the cylinder several times)
- o Tape
- o Pen or marker

Step-by-Step Guide:
1. Find Your Cylinder: Start by finding a cylindrical object around the house. This will be the core of your Scytale. It could be a rolling pin, a thick marker, or even a cardboard tube.
2. Prepare Your Paper Strip: Cut a long strip of paper. It should be narrow enough to wrap around your cylinder and long enough to wrap around several times.
3. Align Your Paper: Begin by aligning the edge of your paper strip with the cylinder's edge. Secure this end with a small piece of tape to keep it in place.
4. Wrap and Write: Gently wrap the strip of paper around the cylinder in a spiral manner, ensuring each new line of the paper slightly overlaps the previous one. The paper should form a neat, angled spiral around the cylinder.
5. Mark Your Message: Now, write your message along the cylinder. Start writing at the edge where the paper begins and write horizontally across the first wrap of the paper. Each word or letter should be on the same line of the spiral. Avoid writing across the edges where the paper wraps to the next layer.
6. Continue the Message: As you reach the end of the first wrap, move to the next layer of the paper spiral and continue writing your message. Keep the words aligned with your first line of text so the message

appears as a series of disjointed letters when the paper is unwrapped.

7. Finish and Secure: Once your message is complete, wrap the remaining paper around the cylinder and secure the end with tape.
8. Unwrap the Mystery: Carefully unwrap the paper from the cylinder. Now, your message will look like a bunch of jumbled letters!
9. Challenge Your Friends: Give your encoded message to a friend and see if they can decode it. They'll need a cylinder of the same size to wrap the paper around and read the message.
10. Decode Messages: When you receive a Scytale message, wrap it around your cylinder to decode it.

Tips for Success:

o Make sure the cylinder's diameter is the same for both encoding and decoding the message.
o Write clearly and evenly as you wrap the paper around the cylinder.
o Experiment with different cylinder sizes for more complex codes.

Safety in Code: Remember, while secret messages are fun, they should always be used for good. No sending mean or hurtful messages – we're all about positive vibes and fun challenges!

WHY CODE ROCK

Playing with codes is fun and also sharpens your brain! It improves problem-solving skills, introduces basic coding concepts, and helps you better understand languages.

Is it time for you to get ready to step into the world of secret codes and hidden messages? Grab your pen and paper, and start coding some super-secret notes! You might just discover you have a knack for languages and coding!

COSMIC VOYAGERS: EXPLORING THE STARLIT SKIES

Get ready, star explorers! After cracking codes and unraveling ancient secrets, it's time to aim our sights even higher: to the stars! Astronomy and stargazing are a fantastic adventure filled with cosmic stories, where every star and constellation has its own tale. Follow me to embark on a stellar journey to learn about the night sky.

STARGAZING: GAZING THROUGH TIME

Let me present the ancient and awe-inspiring practice of stargazing! Since the dawn of time, humans have looked up at the night sky with wonder and curiosity. As you can see, stargazing is not a modern hobby but a journey through history, connecting us with our ancestors who also marveled at the stars.

- o **The Ancient Astronomers:** Our story began thousands of years ago. Ancient civilizations like the Babylonians, Greeks, Egyptians, and Mayans were fascinated by the heavens. They were the original stargazers, charting the stars, planets, and constellations, trying to make sense of the cosmos.
- o **Egyptian Cosmos (3100 BC to 30 BC):** In the land of pyramids and pharaohs, the ancient Egyptians looked to the skies with a reverence that shaped their civilization. The Egyptians meticulously charted the stars, especially those in the Orion constellation, believing them to be linked to Osiris, the god of the afterlife. The alignment of their pyramids, particularly the Great Pyramid of Giza, with specific stars underscores their advanced understanding of astronomy.
- o **Babylonian Brilliance (1894 BC to 539 BC):** The Babylonians, one of the earliest civilizations to dive deep into the mysteries of the night sky, laid the groundwork for future astronomical studies. They meticulously documented the movements of celestial bodies, creating detailed star catalogs and pioneering the practice of systematic observation. The Babylonian legacy in astronomy is perhaps best encapsulated in their development of the zodiac system, a concept that still resonates in the world of astronomy and astrology today.
- o **Greek Galaxies (8th century BC to the 2nd century AD):** The Greeks took the baton of astronomical inquiry from the Babylonians, propelling it into the realms of philosophy and science. Figures like Aristotle and Ptolemy pondered the mechanics of the Cosmos, developing theories and models that, while not

entirely accurate by modern standards, were groundbreaking for their time. The constellations named by the Greeks and the stories attached to them have become an enduring part of our cultural heritage in stargazing.

- o **Mayan Marvels (250 AD to 900 AD):** The Mayans, known for their advanced astronomical knowledge, meticulously observed celestial movements. They created sophisticated calendars, predicting solar and lunar eclipses with remarkable accuracy. Their observatories, like the one at Chichen Itza, are a testament to their deep connection with the cosmos.
- o **First Nations of the North:** Farther north, the indigenous peoples of what is now Canada also had rich astronomical traditions. The Inuit, for example, used the stars for navigation and had their constellations. At the same time, the Plains cultures aligned their ceremonial structures, like medicine wheels, with the sun and stars, marking seasons and celestial events.
- o **Guiding Stars:** For ancient sailors, stars were more than just twinkling lights; they were vital navigation tools. Stars like the North Star (Polaris) in the northern circumpolar constellation of Ursa Minor helped them find their way across vast oceans long before the compass was invented.
- o **Mythology and Legends:** Every culture has star stories and myths, turning constellations into legendary heroes, creatures, and gods. These tales were passed down through generations, making the stars a part of our shared human heritage.
- o **The Birth of Modern Astronomy:** With the invention of the telescope in the 17th century, stargazing entered a new era. Astronomers like Galileo, Copernicus, and Maria Cunitz made groundbreaking discoveries. Maria Cunitz, often overlooked, was one of the most notable astronomers of her time. A Silesian astronomer, she significantly improved upon the planetary theories of Johannes Kepler. She published a comprehensive astronomical table, "Urania propitia," which simplified Kepler's calculations and was widely acclaimed for its accuracy. Her work demonstrated that the universe was far more vast and wondrous than anyone had imagined.

Stargazing is a timeless activity that connects us with the past, present, and future. It's a reminder of our small place in the vast universe and the endless mysteries waiting to be discovered. So, as we look up at the night sky, let's remember the countless stargazers who came before us, sharing in the timeless wonder of the stars.

LET'S STARGAZE! OUR JOURNEY AMONG THE STARS

We can start a cosmic adventure exploring the wonders of the night sky with our celestial neighbor to the distant galaxies. All of them tell a story. The most familiar sights and venture into the vast space are the ones closest to our planet:

1. The Moon. Our Closest Celestial Neighbor:

The Moon is Earth's only natural satellite. It's made of rock, much smaller than Earth, orbiting us and lit by the Sun. Craters, valleys, and dark plains mark the Moon's surface.

- **What to stargaze:** Watch the Moon go through its phases, from a New Moon to a Full Moon. Occasionally, you can witness a lunar eclipse.
- **Interesting Fact:** We call it "The Moon" because, for a long time, humans didn't know other moons existed until Galileo discovered Jupiter's four moons in 1610.

2. The Sun. The Heart of Our Solar System:

The Sun is a star at the center of our Solar System. It's a massive ball of hot, glowing gases, primarily hydrogen and helium, undergoing nuclear fusion. The Sun provides the light and energy that sustains life on Earth.

- **What to stargaze:** You can observe the Sun's changes, like sunspots, using special solar filters or during a solar eclipse. But remember, looking directly at the Sun with your naked eye or through a telescope without proper solar filters can cause severe eye damage.
- **Interesting Fact:** The Sun is not only the heart of our Solar System but also a traveler in space. It, along with the entire Solar System, orbits the center of the Milky Way galaxy. This journey takes approximately 230 million years to complete.

3. The Solar System. Our Cosmic Neighborhood:

The Solar System includes the Sun and what orbits around it, like planets, asteroids, comets, etc. It's a vast expanse, with Earth being one of the eight planets in this system. Do you know how to differentiate planets from stars in the night sky? Easy! Stars twinkle, but planets don't!

- **What to stargaze:** With the naked eye, you can see some planets like Venus and Mars. Binoculars or a small telescope will reveal Jupiter's moons and Saturn's rings. You can also stargaze meteor showers like the Perseids and Geminids, which are spectacular to watch. These "shooting stars" are best seen on clear, dark nights away from city lights.
- **Interesting Fact:** Jupiter is the planet that has the most moons in our Solar System, with a current count of 79.

4. Constellations. Patterns in the Stars:

Constellations are groups of stars that form figures and patterns. Throughout history, these patterns have received different names. They are like celestial landmarks, helping us navigate the night sky.

- **What to stargaze:** Start with learning about major constellations like the Ursa Mayor, Ursa Minor, and Orion. Each has its own set of stars and mythological stories. They're like the main characters in our night sky story; each constellation has a story rooted in mythology. For example, with his belt of three bright stars, Orion the Hunter is one of the most famous tales.
- **Interesting Fact:** There are 88 officially recognized constellations covering the entire night sky. The largest constellation is Hydra, which spans over 3% of the night sky.

5. Galaxies. Cities of Stars

Galaxies are vast collections of stars, dust, gas, and dark matter bound together by gravity. They come in various shapes and sizes, including spiral, elliptical, and irregular forms. The Milky Way, our galaxy, is a spiral one.

- **What to stargaze:** With a good telescope, you can observe some nearby galaxies, like Andromeda, the closest spiral galaxy to us, which is visible as a faint smudge of light under dark skies. The Magellanic Clouds, two small galaxies orbiting the Milky Way, are

128

visible from the Southern Hemisphere. Observing galaxies can give us a glimpse into the vastness of the universe and our place within it.

- **Interesting Fact:** The Hubble Space Telescope has estimated there are more than two trillion galaxies in the universe, each containing millions to trillions of stars.

STARGAZING TIPS:

- Bring Along Your Star Squad: Always have a grown-up, like a parent or teacher, when you're stargazing. It's more fun and way safer that way! If you're with friends, stay close and pick a spot to meet in case you get separated. It's like having a secret meeting point.
- Find Your Starry Guide: Use a star map or a stargazing app to help locate constellations. It's like having a treasure map that guides you through the starry sea.
- Choose Your Star Base Wisely: Find a calm, open spot like your backyard, a nearby park, or a special stargazing field. Just make sure it's away from busy streets and it's a place where you can chill safely.
- Be a Nighttime Ninja: Since we're exploring in the dark, bring a flashlight with a red cover (it helps keep your night vision super sharp!). Watch your step and know what's around you; we don't want any trips or slips!
- Dress Like a Space Explorer: Check the weather and dress like you're ready for a space mission. If it's chilly, bundle up. If it's warm, keep it cool. And if it looks like rain or a storm, let's save our adventure for another night.
- Bring Binoculars: While many constellations are visible to the naked eye, binoculars can help you see more details, like the craters on the Moon or the colors of different stars. If you're using cool gadgets like telescopes or binoculars, ensure you know how to use them. Ask your grown-up star guide for help if you need it.
- Be a Wildlife Whisperer: If we're out in nature, remember we're not alone. There might be animals around, so let's be respectful, keep our noise down, and try not to disturb them.
- Love Your Space: Let's leave no trace behind. That means we keep our stargazing spot as we found, respecting nature and the universe.
- Keep a Stargazing Journal: Write down or draw what you see. It's a great way to track your astronomical journey and the changes in the night sky.

Astronomy is much more than identifying celestial bodies; we can start connecting with the universe and realizing our place in this vast cosmic space. Open your eyes to the skies and uncover the universe's wonders, one star at a time!

MYSTERY MASTERS: DETECTIVE ADVENTURES

Are you ready to transform yourself into a Mystery Master? In this super cool section, we will create our very own detective adventures. Imagine you're in a world filled with hidden clues, secret codes, and mysterious puzzles just waiting to be solved by you. Grab your detective gear and start crafting some mind-boggling mysteries you and your friends can unravel. It's time to unleash your inner detective and dive into a world of intrigue and fun!

WOMEN WHO PIONEERED THE MYSTERY WORLD

But before that, let's take a peek into the exciting world of detective stories and meet some incredible women who made history with their sharp minds and daring adventures. First, we have **Agatha Christie**, a genius writer who created some of the most extraordinary detectives ever, like Hercule Poirot and Miss Marple. Her books are like a treasure hunt, filled with twists and turns that'll keep you guessing! Then, meet **Kate Warne**, a real-life detective wonder. She was the first female detective in America, cracking cases and solving mysteries for the famous Pinkerton Agency. Imagine being a detective in a world where no one expected a woman to be one; that was Kate! And don't forget about **Sara Paretsky**, the writer who brought us V.I. Warshawski, a fearless and super-smart female detective. These fantastic ladies proved that the mystery and detective work world is perfect for anyone who loves a good puzzle and a bit of adventure!

MYSTERY MAKER'S GUIDE: CRAFTING YOUR DETECTIVE ADVENTURE

Are you ready to put all your incredible skills to the test and create your very own mystery adventure? You've already mastered cracking codes and making Spartan scytales, and you're pretty savvy with a compass, too; plus, you know much about stars and constellations and are a pro at camping and outdoor explorations. Let's use all these superb skills to craft an epic mystery!

- Creating Your Mystery: Dream up a super fun and intriguing mystery. Maybe it's a hidden treasure, a coded message, or something mysterious in your neighborhood. Jot down your ideas: who's involved, what's missing, and all the curious happenings. Unleash your imagination to make the story as wild and wondrous as possible. For a twist, try Sequential Storytelling with your siblings or friends: each person adds a part to the story, like passing a baton in a relay race. You write the beginning; a friend adds the next part, and so on. The story grows with each person's imagination, and the final mystery surprises everyone!
- Planting Clues: Now for some sneaky fun! Use secret codes, puzzle pieces, or special objects as clues. Get your parents or friends to help hide them in clever spots around your home or yard. If friends are involved, ensure they're part of the Sequential Storytelling to keep the mystery alive. The best clues make you think; you might even use your compass or star knowledge!
- Puzzles and Riddles: Spice up your mystery with brain-teasing puzzles or riddles. Ask a friend or your parents to add these challenges to be solved for the next clue. They could be word games, math problems, or something that needs a bit of creative thinking. The more variety, the merrier!
- Map Out Your Adventure: As you solve the mystery, use your compass to create a map of locations where each clue and puzzle can be found. Add symbols or codes to your map for an extra layer of mystery. This map is your secret guide to unraveling the adventure.
- Gather Your Detective Tools: Equip yourself like a pro detective. Grab a notebook for clues, hypotheses, and observations, a magnifying glass for inspecting evidence, your compass, a map, and maybe a camera for capturing your findings.
- Solve the Mystery: It's adventure time! Follow the clues, solve the puzzles, and piece together the mystery. Keep an open mind and discuss your findings with your team or family. A good detective considers all possibilities.
- Share Your Story: After cracking the case, it's showtime! Share your thrilling adventure with friends or family. You could write a story, create a mini-book, act out your mystery, or even draw a comic strip or storyboard about your detective journey.

IDEAS FOR MYSTERY'S ADVENTURES

We have two special mystery ideas for you and your friends to start your detective game!

The Case of the Hidden Code

- **The Mystery:** Our beloved school mascot, a cute plush owl named Hootie, has mysteriously disappeared! The only clue left behind is a strange note with a series of symbols and a piece of string. It looks like a secret code! Can you help find Hootie?
- **Your Mission:** Use your detective skills to decode the message and discover where Hootie is hidden. You must create the code using Sequential Storytelling or ask your parents for help. Here's what you need to do:

    1. **Decode the Message:** The note you found is written in a secret code. Use your knowledge of creating and decoding secret messages to figure out what it says. Maybe it's a simple letter substitution or something more complex like a Scytale!
    2. **Follow the Clues:** Once you've decoded the message, it will lead you to different places. Maybe it's a riddle pointing to the library or a clue hidden in the playground. Keep your eyes peeled for more hints!
    3. **Solve the Puzzle:** You might find puzzle pieces as you follow the clues. Put them together to reveal a picture or a final message leading you to Hootie.

The Case of the Lost Treasure of Queen Cleo-Cat-Ra

- **The Mystery:** Queen Cleo-Cat-Ra, the legendary feline ruler of Ancient Kitty-Egypt, had a famous treasure; it was the meow of legends. But, oh no! The treasure map has been torn into pieces and scattered. Can you help piece together the map and find the treasure?
- **Your Mission:** Embark on a thrilling quest to find the pieces of the treasure map and discover where Queen Cleo-Cat-Ra's treasure is hidden. You must create the code using Sequential Storytelling or ask your parents for help. Here's your game plan:

132

1. **Gather the Map Pieces:** Hidden around your home or yard are pieces of the treasure map. Each piece has a part of the map and a puzzle or riddle related to ancient Egypt or cats. Solve these to find the next piece.
2. **Assemble the Map:** Once you've collected all the pieces, it's time to assemble the map. It's like a jigsaw puzzle; each piece will fit perfectly to reveal the treasure's secret location.
3. **Decipher the Clues:** The map is full of mysterious Egyptian symbols. Use your knowledge of secret codes and hieroglyphics to decipher them. They will guide you to the treasure's hiding spot.
4. **Embark on the Final Quest:** Follow the map to explore different locations. Maybe you'll have to measure like an Egyptian architect or walk like an Egyptian to find the next clue.
5. **Find the Treasure:** Use all the clues from the map to discover where Queen Cleo-Cat-Ra's treasure is hidden. Is it buried under the "Sphinx's Paw" (a particular tree or rock in your yard) or hidden in the "Pyramid of Play" (a fort or playhouse)?

Remember:

- Stay safe and let an adult know about your detective game.
- Work together with your friends. Teamwork makes the mystery-solving dream work!
- Keep a notebook handy to jot down your clues and ideas.

Adventure Chronicles

Are you ready to take your adventures to the next level? This section is about expressing yourself and capturing the magic of your journeys. Whether you're a budding writer, a future photographer, or a journaling enthusiast, a whole world of creativity is waiting for you.

Crafting Tales of Adventure and Mystery

In Chapter 5, you became authors with "My Storybook Adventure," creating your own magical worlds. It is the moment to take your storytelling to new heights by weaving tales of outdoor adventures, mystery-solving, and stargazing. Here's how you can infuse your stories with the excitement of your real-life experiences and discoveries:

1. **Adventure Awaits:** Think about your outdoor adventures, maybe a camping trip or a stargazing night. Imagine a story where your characters embark on a similar

journey. What unexpected challenges do they face? Maybe they get lost and must use their compass skills to find their way back or discover a hidden cave with ancient secrets.

2. **Mystery and Intrigue:** Draw inspiration from the detective work you've done. Create a story where your characters solve a neighborhood mystery. They could use secret codes, follow clues, and crack puzzles. Maybe they uncover a historical mystery linked to the stars, combining your stargazing knowledge with detective skills.

3. **Starry Tales:** Use your knowledge of constellations and celestial events to create a story set in the stars. Perhaps your characters embark on a space adventure, visiting different planets and constellations. They could learn about other cultures' star myths or even witness a spectacular meteor shower that changes their perspective.

4. **Character Development:** Remember the characters you created in "My Storybook Adventure"? Let's bring them into these new settings. How would they react to camping in the wild or solving a mystery? Maybe one of your characters is really into astronomy and guides the adventure with their stargazing knowledge.

5. **Sensory Descriptions:** Use your outdoor experiences to enrich your story with sensory details. Describe the smell of the forest, the sound of waves at the beach, or the chill of a night under the stars. These details will make your story more immersive and engaging.

6. **Illustrate Your Adventure:** Just like in "My Storybook Adventure," bring your story to life with illustrations. Draw scenes from your outdoor adventures, mysterious clues, or the starry night sky. Your drawings will add a personal touch and visual excitement to your story.

7. **Share Your Adventure:** Once your story is complete, share it with friends and family. You could even organize a storytelling evening under the stars.

Remember, your adventures and experiences are a treasure trove of inspiration; use them to craft stories that are uniquely yours, filled with the thrill of exploration, the intrigue of mysteries, and the wonder of the cosmos. Let your imagination run, and have fun!

PHOTOGRAPHY FUN: CAPTURING ADVENTURES THROUGH YOUR LENS

Time to capture the world around you in snapshots! Photography is one of my personal favorite hobbies. It is about imagination and telling a story through images.

Whether on a camping trip, solving mysteries, or gazing at the stars, your camera is your tool to freeze those moments in time. Let me share how to use photography to bring your adventures to life!

Photography Basics: Light and Composition for Young Shutterbugs

Understanding light and composition can turn your photos from good to great, even if you're just using a smartphone camera. Here are some simple and fun tips to get you started:

1. Chasing the Light:

- o **Golden Hour:** It is the time before sunset when the light is soft and golden. It's perfect for taking warm, glowing photos.
- o **Shadows and Highlights:** Notice how light creates shadows and highlights. Play with these contrasts in your photos. Early morning or late afternoon light creates longer shadows and can add drama to your images.
- o **Avoid Harsh Midday Sun:** The midday sun can be too bright, causing harsh shadows. If you're taking photos at this time, try finding a shady spot or use a piece of white paper to reflect light softly onto your subject.

2. Composition Fun:

- o **Rule of Thirds:** Imagine your photo divided into nine segments. Try to position the essential parts of your image in your scene at the points where they intersect. It makes the photo more balanced and exciting.
- o **Framing:** To frame your subject, use natural frames like tree branches, windows, or doorways. This focuses attention on the main subject and adds depth to the photo.
- o **Leading Lines:** Use lines like paths, streams, or fences to lead the eye into the picture. It's a great way to create a sense of depth and make your photos more engaging.

3. Getting Creative:

- o **Perspective Play:** Try taking photos from different heights and angles. What does the world look like from the ground or from above?

- o **Reflections:** Use water, fountains, mirrors, or reflective surfaces to create artistic photos.
- o **Fill the Frame:** Get close to your subject so it fills the frame. This can be a fun way to focus on details and textures.

4. Practice Makes Perfect:

- o **Experiment:** The best way to learn photography is by taking many photos. Try different settings, compositions, and subjects. See what works and what doesn't.
- o **Review Your Photos:** Look at your photos and think about what you like about them and what you could improve next time.

Remember, these rules are just guidelines. The most important thing is to have fun and let your creativity shine through your photos. So, start exploring the world through your lens!

SNAPSHOT ADVENTURES

- o **Adventure Photography:** Your outdoor adventures are the perfect opportunity for some fantastic photos. Capture the beauty of nature, the excitement of setting up a tent, or the joy of roasting marshmallows. Try different angles: a close-up of a marshmallow on a stick or a wide shot of your campsite. Each photo tells a part of your adventure story.
- o **Mystery in Photos:** Remember the mysteries you solved? How about recreating some scenes for a photo story? You could photograph a series of clues or stage a photo of you in detective mode, magnifying glass in hand. These photos can be a fun way to remember the mystery you unraveled.
- o **Stargazing Shots:** Capturing the night sky can be challenging but rewarding. If you have a camera that allows manual settings, try long exposure shots to capture stars. Don't worry if your camera can't do this; you can still photograph the Moon or create a photo series of your stargazing setup with telescopes and star maps.

WRAP-UP

How cool was it to learn all those camping tricks and outdoor skills? We became nature detectives with our scavenger hunts, navigated like pros with compasses, and cracked some seriously tricky codes. And didn't we just love gazing at the stars and creating our own detective stories?

Learning how to get snapshots of your adventures was also fun. Aysel and Shani enjoy taking pictures every time we adventure outdoors. We know we are creating memories that will last forever. Remember, every adventure we had and every mystery we solved helped us put our skills into action. I can't wait to see you use these skills to create your own adventure tales!

CONCLUSIONS

Hey there, my wonderful girls! As we come to the end of our journey through this book, I can't help but feel a burst of pride and excitement for all the incredible things we've learned together. Each chapter has been a stepping stone, gaining new skills and growing into confident, capable young women ready to take on the world.

Remember how we started in Chapter 1, learning about the essentials of home and survival skills? Just like you, Aysel and Shani began their journey in the kitchen, a little hesitant at first with the whisk and the frying pan. But oh, how they've grown! Just like you! Aysel's first perfectly cracked egg and Shani's beaming smile, when she mastered the running stitch in sewing are moments I cherish. They remind me of the joy and pride you must feel as you conquer these skills, too.

As we moved through the chapters, tackling financial literacy, STEM, sports, and more, I know how those skills will help you spark your curiosity and strengthen your confidence. Whether it was setting up a lemonade stand, coding your first program, or scoring a goal in soccer, you were not just learning skills but discovering your passions.

In Chapter 6, when we explored leadership, I saw in Aysel and Shani the same potential I see in each of you. Their voices grew stronger, their ideas bolder, and their spirits kinder. They learned, as I hope you have, that being a leader isn't just about being in charge; it's about caring, sharing, and making a positive impact.

And then came the adventures and explorations of Chapter 9. Just like you, Aysel and Shani embarked on outdoor escapades, looked up at the stars with wonder, and crafted their own stories. Their laughter and excitement on these adventures were a reminder of the joy and amazement that await you in every new experience.

Do you remember the section on cryptography? I remember the day we decided to create our own Spartan scytales; it was an adventure in itself!

We gathered around the dining table, armed with paper, scissors, and a sense of mystery. As we rolled the paper around the sticks, forming our ancient encoding devices, I saw their eyes light up with excitement. The real fun began when we started writing secret messages to each other. Aysel and Shani quickly learned the technique of encoding and decoding messages with growing enthusiasm. It wasn't just a lesson in history or cryptography; it was a bonding moment, shared discovery, and unlocking new ways to communicate. It's these moments of discovery and joy that I hope you experience, too, as you explore the pages of this book and the adventures of your own life.

Girls, as you close this book, remember that it's not just a collection of chapters and skills. It's a space to help you grow your abilities to allow you to unfold dreams and your boundless potential. Like Aysel and Shani, you are on a path to discovering your talents, improving your skills, and living a life filled with joy, learning, curiosity, and amazement.

Carry these lessons close to your heart, and let them guide you as you cook, create, explore, lead, and dream because you are not just preparing for the future; you are shaping it with every new skill you master and every new challenge you embrace.

So go ahead, my amazing girls, step into each day with confidence and curiosity. The world is waiting for you to leave your mark, and I can't wait to see where your journey takes you. Keep shining, keep learning, and remember you are extraordinary!"

ABOUT THE AUTHOR

Say hello to Solange Márquez Espinoza, a lawyer and political scientist with a big heart and an even bigger imagination! Born in Mexico, choosing Canada as her home, and Latin at heart, Solange has always cherished stargazing, exploring the ocean, writing stories, and enjoying a good book with hot cocoa.

Solange is deeply passionate about helping girls discover their talents and potential. She loves sharing fun facts and captivating stories with friends just like you. A mother to her 9-year-old twin daughters, Aysel and Shani, who chose her and Paco (their dad) as their guides in this world, Solange balances her time between writing for newspapers, stargazing, and discussing global issues.

In "Girl's Skills for Life," Solange invites you on a fantastic adventure to explore and master various incredible skills. Her dream? To inspire you to explore, dream, and discover the world around you – all while having a blast!

"Girl's Skills for Life" is not just a book; it's a journey into the heart of your potential, guided by the insightful Solange Márquez Espinoza. Designed for girls ready to explore, learn, and grow, this book is a vibrant exploration of skills and life lessons that await you.

Dive into the pages and explore an exciting world where every skill is a step towards becoming your best self. From the excitement of sports to the wonders of the Cosmos, from the art of storytelling to the balance of yoga, your adventure toward excellence begins here.

With Solange's heartwarming tales and practical advice, you'll find encouragement to dream big, celebrate your uniqueness, and embrace the extraordinary journey of life.